Teaching English Language Learners

Teaching English Language Learners

A Handbook for Elementary Teachers

Ann Morgan

ROWMAN & LITTLEFIELD
Lanham • Boulder • New York • London

Published by Rowman & Littlefield
An imprint of The Rowman & Littlefield Publishing Group, Inc.
4501 Forbes Boulevard, Suite 200, Lanham, Maryland 20706
www.rowman.com

6 Tinworth Street, London SE11 5AL, United Kingdom

British Library Cataloguing in Publication Information Available

Library of Congress Cataloging-in-Publication Data

Names: Morgan, Ann, 1954- author.
Title: Teaching English language learners : a handbook for elementary teachers / Ann Morgan.
Description: Lanham : Rowman & Littlefield, [2019] | Includes bibliographical references and index.
Identifiers: LCCN 2018040578 (print) | LCCN 2018049039 (ebook) | ISBN 9781475843880 (Electronic) | ISBN 9781475843866 | ISBN 9781475843866 (cloth : alk. paper) | ISBN 9781475843873 (paper : alk. paper)
Subjects: LCSH: English language—Study and teaching (Elementary)—Foreign speakers.
Classification: LCC PE1128.A2 (ebook) | LCC PE1128.A2 M5594 2019 (print) | DDC 372.652/1044—dc23
LC record available at https://lccn.loc.gov/2018040578

Printed in the United States of America

This work is dedicated to teachers and students of the English language.

Contents

Acknowledgments

I am enormously grateful to the smart, generous people who added to this book and bravoed the project.

My remarkable and encouraging family—Ellen, Peter, and Annalisa—with extra thanks to Peter and Ellen for many years of help with classroom projects and presentations.

The positive, kind, and skilled classroom, ESOL, and administrative professionals whom I so admire and whose insights added in ways untold to my career and this work—Jennifer Shin Ahn, Dawn Audibert, Deborah Becker, Laura Bernard-Sanchez, Linda Bernard, Diane Coffman, Nancy Craig, Katherine Gull, Linda Jordan, Janet Lasky, Colleen Loomis, Julie Lowe, Jerry Perlet, Melissa Ruben, Jennifer Seidel, Avis Silver, Leslie Shear, Erica Valenstein, Janiel Wagstaff, Robb Wainwright, Linda Weiss, Amanda Zammillo, and Raeda Zeitoon

Special recognition to the people and organizations who provided feedback and/or further expertise:

Lyla Combs, CEO and cofounder, Global Center for Refugee Education and Science
Dr. Ellen (Aileen) Curtin, Texas Weslyan University
Dr. Robert A. Fradkin, University of Maryland at College Park
Howard Gardner, Harvard University
Indiana Department of Education, Office of English Language Learning and Migrant Education
Pete Morgan-Dimmick, art
Andrea Nichols, art
Student Handouts, Free Educational Materials for K–12 Teachers and Students of All Subjects
Janiel Wagstaff, Literacy Matters

Acronym Soup and Other Confusing Terms

There is more than enough jargon about English language acquisition, but the following acronyms and terms are the ones that classroom teachers may need to know.

In alphabetical order:

Accommodations - Accommodations are changes in presentation, timing, seating, workload, product, or other interaction between the student and learning environment. Accommodations are meant to make material more accessible to the English learner and to provide a more realistic picture of what the student knows. Federal law requires appropriate accommodations for all English Language Learners, usually based on input from the student's teachers, the English-acquisition specialist, and other professionals as determined by the school administration. Schools work within their state rules for assigning, recording, and using accommodations. Federal law allows individual states to decide if students who have exited formal ESOL programs may or may not continue to get limited accommodations. Individual accommodations are reviewed and revised at the beginning of each school year.

BICS - Basic Interpersonal Communication Skills are playground/lunchroom/video game/TV language skills that are enough for the student to communicate with other kids. Kids pick this up fairly easily from their peers and can speak socially within months or even just a few weeks of arrival in school and have mastery within two years. BICS are informal, mostly oral language, and usually require about three thousand words.

CALPs - Cognitive Academic Language Proficiencies are the "hard stuff" of academic language that include grammar rules, mechanics, content vocabulary, and all those tricky details of academic understanding. Mastery can take anywhere from seven to ten years, particularly in writing. CALPs are formal, complex, usually based on writing, and require hundreds of thousands of words.

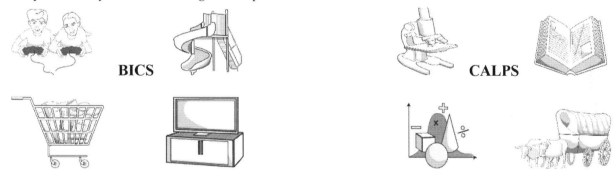

Concurrent Bilingual - A concurrent bilingual is a person who learns two languages simultaneously, starting before the age of two. These kids are equally at ease in both languages. They can switch very easily and quickly from one language to the other.

Consecutive Bilingual - A consecutive bilingual is a person who learns a second language while still a toddler/preschooler, immediately after having learned their first language. Kids usually use one language as easily and as readily as the other.

Domains - Domains are the four major areas of language acquisition. In order of typical mastery, they are:

1. Listening
2. Speaking
3. Reading
4. Writing

EFL - English as a Foreign Language is an English language acquisition program in places where English is not the primary or official language.

EL/ELL - An English Learner or English Language Learner is a person whose first or primary language is not English and who is in an English language acquisition program.

ELT - English Language Training or Teaching describes programs for people preparing to be English language teachers.

ENL - (limited use) English as a New Language is a program for English Language Learners, used in some areas instead of ESL or ESOL.

ESL - English as a Second Language is a program for English learners, but is a misnomer, as many people learn English as a third, fourth, or later language.

ESOL - English for Speakers of Other Languages is a program for English Language Learners.

FEP - Fluent English Proficient students have a lot of English language skills and almost always use them correctly. These students understand and are easily understood by native English speakers.

L1 - Language One is the primary language, the first language a person hears and speaks. It's the go-to language.

L2 - Language Two is the language that a person learns after the first language.

LEP - Limited English Proficient students have a working base for using English, if not always correctly. These students usually understand and are most often understood by native English speakers, despite some vocabulary, pronunciation, and grammar mistakes.

Modifications - Modifications are changes made to the material being taught to make it more accessible to the learner. Most ESOL students do not receive formal instructional modifications.

NEP - Non-English Proficient students have very few English language skills, do not understand the language around them, and are not able to use English to make themselves understood most of the time.

PBL - Project-Based Learning uses theme-based projects to teach content and skills. PBL gives English Learners common experiences on which to build new language.

Plug-in or Push-in Program - Plug-in English language teachers work with the students in their classrooms during content instruction or practice, using the classroom instructional materials.

Productive Skills - Productive skills are active language output that the person creates by speaking and writing.

Pullout Program - Pullout teachers work with English Language Learners in a dedicated space at a regular designated time with instructional materials designed for language acquisition.

Receptive Skills - Receptive skills are passive language input that the person takes in through listening and reading.

REL - A Reassigned English Learner is a student who has officially exited an English language acquisition program. Federal law allows each state to decide if this group of students is eligible for accommodations.

Silent Stage or Phase - The Silent Stage is the period of time when a new student is getting used to hearing a different language and does not speak. The student is often attentive and responsive, but does not talk or speaks only in very short, infrequent fragments. The Silent Stage can be as brief as a few days to as long as, but rarely longer than, a school year.

TESOL - Teachers of English for Speakers of Other Languages is a degree program as well as an international professional organization for English language teachers.

TPR - Total Physical Response is a way for English learners to demonstrate learning by using their bodies or gestures—moving from one place to another, gesturing, pointing, acting out a word or words, nodding, or other physical movement.

World English - World English is English used in different parts of the world. It often sounds markedly different from American English and can be hard to understand. World English speakers have what American English speakers think of as heavy accents and regional vocabulary. World English speakers usually require English language instruction.

Introduction

Quan and Mihn

My first non-English-speaking student in a regular classroom was a second-grader from Vietnam. Quan was thrilled to be in the United States, to be in school, and to have a good meal every day. He was a novelty to everyone in my Title 1 room and we treated him like a treasure. Everybody wanted to be his friend, help him with his work, and shower him with attention. I spoke slowly, in short sentences, with exquisite enunciation. He made remarkable progress, our little hothouse flower, and I gave myself a fairly smug—and premature—pat on the back.

Two months later, Mihn joined the class. Mihn was also from Vietnam, but didn't share Quan's enthusiasm. He was shut down with sadness, anger, and fear—resistant to every interaction. Some of his paperwork indicated "female" and some said "male." Some said he was here with a parent, some said an aunt and uncle. As teacher of record, it was my job to untangle as many of those knots as I could, including the gender question. He was quick to catch on to the ploys of "boys line up here, girls line up there" or taking all-boys or all-girls bathroom breaks. He just didn't line up or go to the bathroom.

The spotlight shifted from Quan to Minh, and I started talking to Quan like he had a Masters in English. After repeated failures with the boy-or-girl question, I finally took the direct route. I just asked Quan. We went into the hall and closed the door. I pointed to myself and said, "I am a girl." Quan agreed, "Oh, yes!" I pointed to him, "You are a boy." More vigorous nodding. I spread my hands and shrugged my shoulders, "Is Minh a girl or a boy?" Quan mimicked my motions and said, "Oh, I no know." The matter remained unresolved for the rest of the school year and for several years after.

And that was my first lesson—*it's all relative.*

Maria

Same school, same grade, different year. By then, the influx of Southeast Asian refugees had become the influx of Central American refugees. Many of my kids had been in English-speaking classrooms for a year or two, so we were able to communicate fairly smoothly. One quiet afternoon, I sat with a reading group at the back of the room while the rest of the students did desk work. There was a commotion in the hall, so I called to a student in the front, "Maria, please close the door," and went back to my reading group. A few minutes later, I did a room scan and asked, "Where is Maria?"

Nobody moved. Nobody answered. I asked again, "Does anyone know where Maria is?" One little voice said, "She in duh hall." My question of "Why?" got me more silence, so I went out into the hall. Maria stood against the wall near the door, sobbing. I was shocked and asked her why she was crying. She couldn't answer me. I asked her why she was in the hall, and her answer broke my heart. "Yoo-ooo s-s-s-say close duh doo-oo-oor!"

I hugged her (it was still allowed) until she caught her breath, and then told her that I wanted her to *stay in the classroom* to close the door. I waited with her until she felt ready to rejoin the group. The class was worried, so I apologized. I told them I had made a mistake and would be more careful when I gave them directions.

Second ESOL lesson—*don't assume that your audience knows what you're talking about.*

Yogi

The final lesson was delivered by a very troubled student during my first year at a new school, my first year teaching third grade. Her name was Yolanda, but she wanted to be called Yogi, and this was her third school in three years. She was the oldest first-generation child of a crowded family from East Africa, but her issues were minimally language and cultural.

On the first day of school, she excused herself to go to the bathroom as the morning bell rang, was gone for twenty minutes, and came back with all her clothes on inside out and backward. It was the start of a hard year for all of us. Yogi could not be controlled and the school was stymied in its efforts to find a better placement for her. She'd use everything and anything as a weapon, bolt from the building, and steal or destroy whatever she could get her hands on.

We had very little communication or cooperation from her non-English-speaking family. Yogi spent most of the year sitting with me at my desk, writing and illustrating horrific blood-letting scenes. I didn't demand any school work; if she was quiet and not hurting anyone, it was a good day. At the end of one not-good day, she was tipping over desks, yelling, throwing things, completely exasperated and exasperating. The buses had already started to pull away, she wouldn't get ready to leave, and I didn't know what to do. I finally asked, "Yogi, what do you want?" She came to a standstill and said, "I want you to help me."

It was a stunning answer. And she was right. I had helped every other kid in the class, I had helped other staff deal with her, I'd helped myself by minimizing expectations for her, but I had not really helped Yogi.

Keep perspective, the most important ESOL lesson for me.

How This Translates to the Teacher

It would be nice if these lessons had provided answers to all my questions about English Language Learners (ELLs) in the elementary classroom. They didn't, but they prompted me to think more broadly when met with a puzzling EL or ESOL situation. My eighteen years as a classroom teacher in a huge metro-like suburban system introduced me to kids and families from every continent except Antarctica. Some kids were very Quan-like, others more Mihn-ish, none were quite like Yogi, and there were many other types in the mix. They stayed with me.

When I shifted to being an English Language specialist in the same school system, the non-English-speaking students who had looked at me hundreds and hundreds of times with hope and expectation came regularly to mind. They helped me help my ESOL students and their classroom teachers.

This isn't a textbook, and I don't want to imply that I know everything. This book is meant to be an at-your-fingertips set of ideas for teachers who want some tried and true strategies to:

- make the most of each day with ESOL students
- work with the ELs' adults
- recognize when English acquisition *isn't* the problem
- provide more instruction without losing more time and energy
- boost kids over writing hurdles
- integrate these kids smoothly into the whole group
- generally make school a successful, happy experience for them

One of the great things about working with this population is that just about everything you do helps. Your ELs learn something every day. You may not know what it is, and it may not be what you wanted from them that day, but it's there and it goes with them. Much of what they take home often helps them adjust to the new culture and language. It's a big deal, and it starts in your confident, productive classroom. Your ESOLers can do it.

Sometimes, though . . .

Miss Rogers and Mrs. Gill, both ESOL teachers, were in small-group rooms across a very narrow hall from each other. The doors lined up, so each could see the other at the front of their respective rooms, and with both doors open, could hear but not see the students.

Mrs. Gill's class had worked on a trees unit every day for two weeks. They had used highly illustrated nonfiction books, gone outside and done bark rubbings, made diagrams, taken pictures, collected leaves — you name it. At the end of the unit, Mrs. Gill did a quick oral review:

Mrs. Gill: What do we call the outside of a tree?

Students: [no response]

Mrs. Gill: It's brown and bumpy. (side eye from Miss Rogers to Mrs. Gill)

Students: [no response]

Mrs. Gill: We put paper on it and rubbed it with crayons. (Miss Rogers rolls her chair to her door and raises her hand, side eye from Miss Gill to Mrs. Rogers)

Students: [no response]

Mrs. Gill: It starts with "b." (Mrs. Gill turns her head to Miss Rogers, who mouths, "BARK.")

One student voice suddenly calls out, "OOH! LADYBUG !!!"

Mrs. Gill hangs her head and takes two steps across the hall to stand in Miss Rogers's door.

Miss Rogers: It's not you.

ONE
Who Are These Kids?

ESOL population statistics may not benefit your daily instruction, but they can help you know that you and your ELs are not alone. The latest information from the US Census shows the following:

- 21 percent of households in the United States speak a language other than English
- 5 million, or 13 percent, of the US population is foreign born (https://www.census.gov/quickfacts/fact/table/US/PST045216)
- There are more than 350 non-English languages spoken in the United States, including Native American languages but not international dialects (https://www.census.gov/data/tables/2013/demo/2009-2013-lang-tables.html)

IDENTIFYING ENGLISH LANGUAGE LEARNERS

When new students register, many systems require that the adult/parent/guardian fill in a form that indicates the language(s) used at home. If any language other than, or in addition to, English is listed, the student should be given an English language screening and placement test. If the form indicates English, look at the family countries of origin to determine if it is American English or World English; World English often requires a language proficiency assessment.

Each state has its own assessment rules, including which one to use and in what time frame. The ESOL specialist in the building or district assumes testing responsibility once he or she is notified of the student's registration and attendance. Kids who are new to the country are usually tested when they go through the district office for international students, so they come to the building already identified and with a recommended level of English language instruction.

It is not unusual for families to indicate that the only language spoken at home is English even when that's obviously not the case. There's an unfortunate negative association among some families that having a child in ESOL somehow tarnishes their record, implies that something is wrong with their baby, or disconnects them from their main learning community. Parents and guardians own the decision about whether or not a child will receive ESOL services, but most are willing to take the advice of classroom teachers, the ESOL specialist, and/or school administration to give ESOL a try.

There are times when the adults and students do speak English, but a regular care provider does not. Sometimes it's a babysitter or a grandparent that the student regularly hears speak a non-English language, but whom the student answers in English. This is a typical transition stage, and even though the kid speaks English, he or she is not used to hearing and listening in English. This is most often a pre-K or Kindergarten situation. These kids should not be overlooked when doing ESOL placement testing, to get an idea of how well they attend to directions and classroom interactions in English.

Sometimes a student has older siblings who have been in the country longer, or who have been through ESOL. It's not unusual for younger siblings not to need ESOL services because they have had better English exposure at home.

If a student's English skills are not enough to keep him or her afloat in classroom instruction, but parents have declined services, document the refusal and whatever difficulties the student may have. Revisit the ESOL question with the adults as soon as there are enough anecdotal records and data to support another recommendation and try to have another teacher or an administrator reinforce the request. A gentle, respectful approach with administrative support at the school, where staff knows the family and student, is the most productive way to allow parents to change their minds.

If they continue to decline services, continue to document, and include notes from your contact with the family. If a child is struggling because of language deficits, that child will miss many of the basics and the gaps he or she started with will only widen. When the problem warrants attention from intervention specialists, the ESOL question will be part of the discussion, so the notes about parent refusal of services will be very important and may keep the classroom teacher out of hot water.

Parents also have the option of pulling their child from ESOL services at any time. Hopefully, there will have been some previous communication between the family and school before this decision. A trusted family friend or teacher should point out the advantages the ESOL program provides to their child (ongoing support, preteaching and reinforcement of classroom skills, a "safe" place for kids to take a break or get social/cultural help, building a community with other English Learners), but again, the family owns the decision. Refusal must be in writing with a signature from the parent or legal guardian, and on record at the school and/or central office.

The school must make it very clear that the child will still have to take the federally mandated end-of-year language progress assessment, and continue to take it annually until the student officially "passes" or exits services. Sometimes, when pulling the student out proves not to be such a great idea after all, parents want to reenter their kids. If this change of heart happens within one year of the date of the parents' written refusal of services, the student may reenter without any further ado. After one year, however, that ship has sailed and the student may not be reentered on the ESOL roster. Given the requirement to take the end-of-year assessment, this can make for some very unhappy parents that are best dealt with by administration.

Most states have guidelines for how long a school may try to get language support for a given student. You can't dance with someone who won't get out of their chair, so sometimes you just have to know when to quit. Check your state's Department of Education website for their parameters.

Countries and Backgrounds

Any country with people has probably had émigré to the United States. ESOL kids come from everywhere except Antarctica, including the United States. Many non-English-speaking young students are second generation, born in the United States, but living in households that function in the first-generation language. Being born in the United States doesn't make a student any less ESOL-needy than one who came over a border. Most schools do not involve themselves with documented or undocumented status or enforcing visa expiration dates, nor is that the responsibility of individual teachers. It's best to check with central administration if there is a school problem or question about immigration status.

Most immigrant populations tend to settle where there are already culturally familiar pieces in place—language, food, religion, family. An American family having to move abroad would do the same thing, finding a place to settle where their culture of birth is accepted and respected. Families want to go to food stores and churches where they can relax and talk easily to people with similar frames of reference. Public transportation is often a part of settlement patterns; a bus line to work or school can be very important.

Sometimes leaving the home country isn't a choice. Political asylees must often go at a moment's notice when danger at home is imminent. There are situations where families are separated if some are traveling and others are at home during such an emergency. Fortunate families are traveling together when they are cautioned not to return home, but it's a trauma nonetheless.

When there is a manmade or natural disaster across the globe, families may be anxious about relatives in that area. Students from affected countries will start arriving in US schools, usually within six months, and usually in metropolitan areas. Their first stop is often temporary, but it behooves us to make the transition to an American school as smooth as possible and to have the student documents correct and ready to go when the student suddenly moves on.

Kids do not always come or stay with an intact family. Find out who the child is living with, who the legally responsible adult is, who came with the student and who did not. If the student is with an aunt, uncle, grandparent, or older sibling, you can refer to the guardian as "your grown-up" rather than as "your parents/mom/dad."

Frequently, one adult comes ahead to get settled, and the rest of the family follows one or two at a time over several years. You can imagine how difficult these long separations must be, and how trying it would be to leave behind familiar places and things to be dropped into an alien land. A student may have been here a while, but those people and things are still missing. Even when a student is glad to live in the United States, has a home, is financially and food secure, has not had trauma, is with loving and caring people, and has had some English language practice, it's hard to move to a foreign country.

A blended international family entered an elementary school that had a broad ESOL population. This family had an unusual mix of some names that were typically Spanish and others that were Scandinavian. The mom was Chilean, had been living in the United States for several years, and had met a Swedish man through her work. When he wasn't traveling, the man had been living with his three children in Sweden but moved his family to the United States after the new marriage. The mom sent for her eight-year-old son, Rico, who had been living in Chile with his paternal grandmother and cousins since his first birthday.

Getting here was the easy part. Getting along here was not. There was no common language in the household; Rico did not want to be living—outnumbered—with all those strangers, nor they with him. He did not accept his mother's or stepfather's authority and could not verbalize his feelings, so he acted them out at home and at school, and on and on and on.

Midyear, they moved to another school district. It was meant to be a secret so the kids wouldn't have to get used to another school, but they had to get up an hour earlier every day to get to the original school on time and, meanwhile, stay quiet about the move. The stress of it all overwhelmed Rico and precluded him being able to cooperate or participate in learning, despite his natural intellectual curiosity and his placement with a kind, skilled, energetic teacher. As is typical when young kids feel like they have no control over their lives, they use the control they have over themselves in eating, sleeping, and bathroom habits. All those things held true for this little guy who just wanted to go home.

Period of Adjustment

This may tap into every management skill a teacher has, and then some. The new-to-the-country ESOL student is undergoing an onslaught to the senses. Things look, sound, smell, taste, and feel funny. It's scary. It's inescapable. The system may tell you to get this newbie up to speed, but your intuitive "kidometer" is bouncing into the red zone. Other things sometimes have to wait while a student finds his or her footing, and like any adjustment, it takes time and depends on individual circumstances.

There may be a "honeymoon period," which is lovely, but be prepared for the newcomer to eventually hit a wall. Sometimes, just when things are looking good, there can be a negative burst of attention from authorities who are looking for undocumented people. This is an enormously scary scenario that affects kids in every way, and which schools must watch out for via student behaviors. School personnel have no power in these cases, but teachers can help young kids feel valued and taken care of.

Grade Placement

Kids coming through the international office are often placed one grade below their age-peers, but this is not always best for the student, particularly past the primary years. If the family understands sufficiently, they may have a say in the student's grade placement. Sometimes a family doesn't know till they get there. If a system doesn't have an international office, the receiving school usually makes placement decisions.

Anastasia, a very small kindergartener, arrived a few weeks into the school year, drenched in tears, and wouldn't get off the bus. She had never been to school, but her parents had declined advice to start her in a half-day pre-K class instead of full-day Kindergarten.

Two days before, she'd been in Russia. The next day, she'd been in a big place with lots of doors and funny-sounding people who gave her shots. The next day, an enormous yellow-orange "busosaurus" came to her house, opened its mouth, swallowed her, and took her away from her tired, weeping parents. It stopped at a different big place with lots of doors and opened its mouth again. The principal managed to get her off the bus, but couldn't get her past the front hall, so she called Miss Rogers, the ESOL teacher—not because she spoke Russian, but because soothing terrified non-English-speaking five-year-olds falls into the "other duties as assigned" ESOL job description.

First stop was the bench under the giant "WELCOME!" sign; let the irony not be lost here. Miss Rogers sat with her arm around Anastasia all morning until Anastasia simultaneously ran out of tears and got hungry. Another teacher brought her a lunch tray, so she had something to eat. By early afternoon, she was too tired to cry except at intervals, but had enough wobble left in her skinny little legs to walk to the nearby bathroom.

This became a daily pattern, with incremental improvements of less crying and more moving: from the bench to the office to the ESOL room to peeking through the window of the Kindergarten room to standing inside the Kindergarten room door until, after a couple of weeks, she reluctantly joined circle time. And you know once you've joined circle time, you're hooked.

A nearby high-school student had been adopted from Russia several years before, and through the Principal Hotline, it was arranged to have this teenager visit Anastasia at school. Anastasia was equal parts shocked and delighted when this lovely young woman sat down next to her in the lunch room and struck up a conversation in Russian. She assured Anastasia that she would be OK and that school wasn't scary.

Anastasia's light went on and stayed on. She proved to be a delightful, clever little girl, despite the pre-K gaps and troubling entry into the system. As Miss Rogers was walking the Kindergarten group to the ESOL room one day, Anastasia skipped ahead and knocked on the locked door. She peeked in, then grinned at Miss Rogers and said, "You not there."

In that same group was a girl from China whose paperwork said she was five years old. She was a head taller than every other Kindergartener and she had most of her second teeth, so the claims of being only one-hand-old were dubious. She was frantically frustrated to be with these babies, and always angry at her parents. At least once a week she would have a rant, "We go to grocy stoh an my muvvuh do evuhthin WONG!" This smart little girl would have had a far easier adjustment to school if we'd had the right information about how old she really was, and the parents had understood that we could place her in a more age-appropriate grade.

There are times when the principal has to direct ESOL traffic. A twelve-and-a-half-year-old girl from Eastern Europe had been adopted into an American family after spending most of her life in an orphanage. She had had a series of intermittent brief stays in foster families in her home country before being adopted. Her new parents wanted her to join the fifth-grade class at the elementary school to help her get used to American school and to avoid the raucous middle-school setting for a few months, so registered her accordingly.

After she'd been at school for a few days, the classroom and ESOL teacher recognized that she was far too mature for elementary school. After they consulted with the administrator, he engaged the Principal Hotline to arrange a meeting with him, the middle-school principal, and the parents. Two days later, she was a middle-schooler, and had avoided being a future fifteen-year-old eighth-grader.

The Silent Stage

New ESOLers may give you the silent treatment as they adjust, but not in "talk to the hand" mode. Language learners acquire new skills in the same pattern that babies learn to talk. First they listen, then they gesture, then they name a few nouns, and then generalize a few verbs, and so on. The most important step in the process is the listening. While new language skills are going in, already acquired skills can be dormant because the language learning "muscles" are busy working on the new stuff. The learner will practice the new stuff in isolation, then wake up the previously acquired skills, pair them with the new stuff, and voila—progress!

That listening part can take a long time for some English Learners and can create worry for the classroom teacher. Kids get pretty adept at making their needs understood without having to say a word, and kind young classmates are always on standby to move things along. What looks like disinterest or distraction or just plain lack of cooperation is most often the ESOLer not understanding, coupled with getting used to the new sounds and mentally practicing them.

You may ask silent students to repeat words, but let it go if they don't comply. They don't want to make mistakes, and the more fearful students are, the longer it will take them to try a word or two. We can tell these EL kids that we know they're smart and we understand if they're not sure about something, that we want to hear what they know, but it doesn't help to force the issue.

In one instance, an anxiety-prone first-grader spoke monosyllables only one-to-one with the ESOL teacher until almost the end of the school year. The ESOL teacher finally told this little boy that he had to show his classroom teacher what a good thinker he was so he could go to second grade. He answered, "I'm really good at math. I help my little brother." This was an overnight success after eight months of silent practice. Some kids don't need silent time at all, others need as much as they can get. In another case, a twelve-year-old girl from Korea was placed in fifth grade and didn't speak until the end of middle school.

Behavior

No experienced teacher will be surprised at how creatively bad some kids can be at school, and probably has a ready arsenal of management skills to keep things on track. For an ESOL student, there can be more at play than what looks like resistance and noncompliance. It helps to get information from other folks who work or have worked with the kid in question. Before contacting the family, consult the building ESOL specialist, read the student's cumulative (cume) and other files, send an email to a previous school, and talk to current building staff who also work with the student. A bigger picture can go a long way toward discerning the "why," and you'll know whether or not it's a good idea to talk to the family.

Classroom teachers can generally overlook or gently manage ESOL behaviors that are directly linked to lack of language comprehension or student stress. ESOL kids want to be like everybody else, but until they are, they're not. When kids feel out of control, they take control of their bodies in ways that warrant attention. For little kids, they can control eating, sleeping, and bathrooming.

Food

Lunches from EL homes often look and smell different, so a kid may eat with his or her face lowered almost into the lunch bag, keep the lunch bag closed and slide pieces out one at a time, not eat, or eat secretly in someplace unobtrusive. Having food in the bathroom is a bad idea, so find an alternative spot as the best short-term response. If the lunchroom is the only option, the classroom and/or ESOL teacher can go in and eat with the student a few times. It may help lunchroom staff to have a heads-up about students new to the country, as the whole cafeteria experience may be unnerving and anxiety-producing for new students. Later in this book there is a description of an easy program called Book Talk that can also help with lunch problems.

Sleep

Who among us hasn't wanted to do a face plant on our desks and snore into the plan book? Kids feel the same way. Lots of ESOL kids live in noisy shared housing, or with adults who have multiple jobs with long hours. Kids keep unusual hours in order to accommodate other schedules. One boy in elementary school used to go to his dad's evening shift at a garage and sleep in a car because his mom worked nights.

Elementary EL students may have tiring responsibilities for younger siblings or cousins. A third-grader was the oldest of a sibling–cousin household with two moms who were sisters. Of necessity, the moms worked and slept at odd hours, so Marco was very often in charge of getting himself, a set of twins in Kindergarten, two first-graders, and a second-grader on the bus every morning and into bed at night. As one of the brothers told the ESOL teacher, "Even duh dog listen to Marco."

The kids shared rooms and beds, kept each other awake, drove each other crazy, and were always wired or tired. If they fell asleep in class, teachers let them sleep. This can't go without parent contact by the classroom teacher, nurse, counselor, ESOL teacher, or administrator; but if a family has few or no options, it is what it is.

Explaining child safety laws is not always effective against economics and culture. In Marco's case, the family was doing the best it could. He spent many lunch or recess periods in the ESOL room or in his classroom, with just the teacher. Lots of times he'd nap, but sometimes he just wanted a quiet break to do his homework, draw, or play by himself.

Bathroom Problems

Bathroom problems are not fun, and usually require intervention by the health specialist in the building. Teachers of young kids are used to occasional accidents and can tell what's an "oops" and what isn't. Most schools have a few unisex changes of clothing available for those moments.

We're all familiar with the serial bathroom-breaker who just wants out, but real bathroom problems are a sign of illness or distress that go beyond the teacher's purview. Frequent accidents, not being able or willing to clean oneself after using the bathroom, deliberately messing oneself and/or the bathroom, or other out-of-the ordinary problems absolutely must be redirected to someone who can work with the family to either train the child in self-care or find other, more significant help. If the family is non-English speaking, the ESOL teacher usually has resources for translators or bilingual counselors who will step in.

Many systems have Language Line (https://www.languageline.com/) subscriptions for interpretations via telephone. The school calls the Language Line, and an operator takes the information about the caller, the language needed, and the purpose of the call. The operator then connects the caller to a bilingual speaker who contacts the family on an open line. There is a real-time conversation between school and home/work, with the Language Line interpreter relaying messages.

Bathroom problems can mean that immediate help is needed from home, and the Language Line serves well if other language help is not available. It's not advisable to have a bilingual student or parent in the building act as interpreter because of confidentiality.

An Adjustment Problem

Much of the stuff ESOL kids do as they adjust can be waited out or massaged into a workable modification. Gregor arrived from Russia in October and was placed appropriately in second grade. He was silent but made a good effort to do some work and interact with his new classmates. He cooperated in every mute way he could but would not take off his jacket.

From the day he arrived, his jacket was zipped up to his chin, with the hood pulled down to his eyebrows, all day, every day. The teacher, Mrs. Lock, was puzzled about his refusal to use the cubbies, but talked to Miss Rogers and decided to leave it alone. The jacket was Gregor's security blanket; it belonged to him, made him feel safe, reminded him he was going to leave eventually, and most importantly, it hid him. It was the outerwear version of the silent stage; he just cocooned in there, being invisible, while he figured things out.

Gregor was bonded to that jacket all the way through April, but eventually he shed it. First the zipper came down an inch at a time over a few weeks until it was open all the way. Then the hood slid back in increments until his whole head was uncovered. Here he hit Jacket Plateau for a while, but he started talking more.

One day he came in with the hood back on his head but took his arms out of the sleeves so the jacket could just hang on him. Finally, as the class was working on a project that required full arm mobility, he simply brushed the jacket off his head and let it hit the floor. The other kids gave Miss Rogers the "DID YOU SEE THAT?" big eyes. She gave them the Smiling-Double-Raised-Eyebrow-Finger-To-Her-Lips response.

Gregor scooped up his jacket when it was time to leave, and the class walked back to their primary classroom. In Gregor went, hung the jacket on the back of his chair, and got to work. Mrs. Lock and Miss Rogers exchanged the same looks that the kids had exchanged with Miss Rogers. It was a Proud Teacher Moment. Within a week, the jacket moved from the chair, to the cubbies, to the closet floor. Gregor was one with the class.

Not an Adjustment Problem

There are times, however, when the issue is obviously just an errant kid and has nothing to do with adjustment to a new environment or language.

Kim came in at the beginning of Kindergarten, one of five kids in an extended family group in grades K–3. She was bright and caught on quickly, but soon went from "I got it!" to "I'm smarter than everybody."

Her teacher, Mrs. White, and her ESOL teacher Miss Rogers double-teamed her on behavior management, but all that did was drive her behaviors underground. They were soon getting reports from other staff and students about the mean things Kim was saying and doing when she thought no one was looking. Conferences with Kim's parents, bilingual counselor, and principal had limited, short-term effect.

Her language skills blossomed, but her social skills were another story. She went into Mrs. Lock's first grade articulate and bossy, and even better at subterfuge. Midway through first grade, when she was supposed to be outside at recess one afternoon, a building service worker found her in a boys' bathroom in the upper-grades wing of the building. Naturally, he walked her to the new assistant principal's office, where Kim superbly played the ESOL card as a newcomer, "I sorry! I lost! I not know!" and so on.

The assistant principal had a generous perspective, so he believed Kim, who went merrily on her way until Mrs. Lock told Miss Rogers about it after school. In the morning, Miss Rogers appeared at her classroom door wearing the "You're In It Deep, Kid" teacher face that prompted Kim to scoot into the cubbie closet. (A pause here to say that ESOL teachers are often the first recourse for repeat offenders, not only because of the myriad of possible circumstances, but because they see the ESOL kids several times a week for years; they have history and, usually, trust.)

Kim spent the morning writing apology notes to the building service worker, the assistant principal, her parents, her teacher, and to Miss Rogers and the grade-one ESOL group for embarrassing them. Then she had to hand-deliver the notes and use her near-perfect oral language skills to explain to each person the purpose of the boy/girl icons on bathroom doors. She's a third-grader now and nothing's changed.

Clothes

Kids from warm climates may not have or be able to get the right clothes for cold weather, including socks, gloves, boots, and other basic winter gear. They often wear piles of T-shirts. They may invent excuses to visit the nurse or hide to avoid going outside. Find a way to let the student stay inside to "help" an adult straighten the class library, sort papers, wash the desks, put away PE equipment, or perform other small tasks. Let them invite a friend to help; it's a wonderful way for kids to relax, develop social connections, and build oral language skills by talking to you and to each other.

School counselors have resources for students needing clothes, so any teacher or the student can check there for needed items. Staff members often have their own kids' outgrown items to contribute to the ESOL room stash. Kids can borrow what they need and either return items (except for hats) or keep them. Send home some kind of signed smiley-face note, so the adults know it's OK.

Realistic Expectations

It's hard to tell early on how well a student will do in their English language journey. It's also hard to tell how adept they are in their first language. If there is background information in school records, it can give a general idea of the family level of education and/or literacy. Family members who have been professionals in their home countries may not yet be able to work at the same level in the United States. Whatever the breadwinner's current job is may not give a true picture of their education, work experience, or expectations for their children.

What is true is that a student with low-level L1 skills will have a hard time learning past that level. Kids who speak incorrectly in their first language have no "hooks" to hang correct new language skills on. It can be done, but it will take a lot of time and extra effort.

The presence of L1 literacy in the home is a good indicator of future literacy in English. Kids who have early, regular exposure to books and other reading materials come to school with an understanding and appreciation of their value.

There are students who have no books at home in their first language, and who do not have the opportunity to get to the public library. Some students have parents who have limited literacy in L1. Classroom teachers perform a great service to these kids by keeping room libraries, doing daily read-alouds, and using Sustained Silent Reading. For ESOL students, read-alouds not only provide academic and cultural reference, but help them get familiar with English structure, pronunciation, inflection, and cadence.

In the author's experience in a large urban-area school district, English Learners clear the Gifted and Talented bar at higher percentages than non-EL students. The screening instrument is nonlanguage based, so they have a better opportunity to demonstrate their thinking skills. Often, they are good thinkers but poor producers because classroom work requires performance that ELs struggle to keep up with. Checking for understanding without the English language barrier allows ESOL students to demonstrate how well they solve problems. They do it all day, every day, and some of them have a long history with it.

Miss Rogers was talking to a fifth-grade boy new to the school, but not new to ESOL. He told her he was from Peru. Miss Rogers said, "That's a long way from here." He answered, "It's a long way to walk."

KEY TAKEAWAYS

- World English warrants a closer look at proficiency.
- Many non-English speakers are born in the United States.
- ELs are identified and leveled with specific, state-chosen placement tests.
- Parents and legal guardians make the final decisions about having their children receive ESOL services.
- Parents and legal guardians may pull their kids from ESOL with a written request that is signed and dated.
- EL students must take the annual progress assessment until their scores warrant official exit from services.
- Global events affect ESOL families and/or spike the ESOL population in the United States.
- Some ESOL students are living without their parents and some of their close family members, and/or in busy shared housing.
- ESOL students need time to adjust and may have some unusual behaviors until they're comfortable, but not all out-of-line behavior is because of language acquisition.
- The school may have to help some ESOL students with lunch, appropriate clothing, and/or personal habits.
- Low skills and literacy in L1 often equate to low skills and literacy in L2/English, and vice-versa.

TWO

Home Comes to School

ESOL students are either the first or second generation in their families to attend American schools. For purposes here, *first generation* refers to students whose parents did not attend school in the United States. *Second generation* refers to students whose parents attended school in the United States, but whose grandparents did not. Both groups have struggles between home and school, but they are somewhat different.

First-generation ELs have one foot in the home culture and are dipping one toe from the other foot into the culture pool of the American school. They are the family trailblazers. It can be a tough job for an elementary student, although some kids seem not to mind, and some even savor it.

The older generations at home, still speaking the home language, often expect their first-generation children to adhere to behaviors and standards of the first culture. Like all other kids, though, they want to blend in at school. To paraphrase a Japanese proverb, "Nail [*sic*] that stick out get pounded." The first-generation student "sticks out" at school, but can be hard-pressed to balance and/or manage the transition between home and school expectations. First-generation school kids are supposed to keep speaking the home language, but also to use their English skills to translate and help the family function in stores, at the doctor's office, and elsewhere in the community.

Second-generation ELs find it a bit easier to bridge their two cultures, but if there are older family members in the house, it may be a little harder to feel fully Americanized. Second-generation ELs have one foot firmly in each culture, and apparently feel comfortable in both. They don't usually need as much English language instruction, especially if they have older second-generation siblings. Most of them have a good understanding of how and why their lives at home and school may demand different behaviors.

One thing that both generations have in common is that they are, for the most part, private about family life. If the family needs help or is in distress of some kind, the ESOLer will not share with the teacher that there is a problem. You'll see it in changed behaviors.

There's a lot going on behind the scenes with ESOL kids. The iceberg diagram (figure 2.1) gives you a glimpse of what you might see and know, and what you probably won't see or know.

It would be impossible to list here every cultural difference that teachers should be aware of, but there are sites online that can help. *The Cultural Crossing Guide* (http://guide.culturecrossing.net/basics_business_student.php?id=11) is one source that can help school staff get a handle on some ELs' behaviors and how best to interact with those students and their families without unintentionally insulting them. Standards are listed by their countries of origin.

GENERAL INFORMATION

1. With rare exception and despite what we may not understand, parents from everywhere love and treasure their children and work hard to do what they believe is best for them.

The Iceberg Concept of Culture

Like an iceberg, the majority of culture is below the surface.

Surface Culture

Above sea level
Emotional load: relatively low

food ▪ dress ▪ music ▪
visual arts ▪ drama ▪ crafts
dance ▪ literature ▪ language
celebrations ▪ games

Deep Culture

Unspoken Rules
Partially below sea level
Emotional load: very high

Unconscious Rules
Completely below sea level
Emotional load: intense

courtesy ▪ contextual conversational patterns ▪ concept of time

personal space ▪ rules of conduct ▪ facial expressions

nonverbal communication ▪ body language ▪ touching ▪ eye contact

patterns of handling emotions ▪ notions of modesty ▪ concept of beauty

courtship practices ▪ relationships to animals ▪ notions of leadership

tempo of work ▪ concepts of food ▪ ideals of childrearing

theory of disease ▪ social interaction rate ▪ nature of friendships

tone of voice ▪ attitudes toward elders ▪ concept of cleanliness

notions of adolescence ▪ patterns of group decision-making

definition of insanity ▪ preference for competition or cooperation

tolerance of physical pain ▪ concept of "self" ▪ concept of past and future

definition of obscenity ▪ attitudes toward dependents ▪ problem-solving

roles in relation to age, sex, class, occupation, kinship, and so forth

Figure 2.1.   Used with permission from the Indiana Department of Education Office of English Language Learning & Migrant Education.

2. Is the student from a matriarchal or patriarchal society? If patriarchal, all major decisions are made by the man of the family. The man of the family may be the father, grandfather, older brother, uncle, or any man who lives with the student. If mothers attend meetings alone, they will nod along, but not agree to or sign anything at the meeting. If both parents attend meetings, the father will do all the talking. Some religions forbid a man to touch any woman not his wife, so he may not shake hands with female staff.

Some patriarchs are not prepared to accept any school authority who is a woman, and meetings can get heated or dead-end. In those cases, it is best to have a male authority figure attend in order to keep things moving. It takes more than a few deep breaths to get past the argument, "But I am the man."

Some cultures are matriarchal and decisions are made by the highest-ranking woman in the family—grandmother, mother, aunt, oldest daughter. In this case, the school must be aware that the matriarch expects deference even at school and particularly in meetings about their child/ren.

3. It's also important to know about discipline practices. Parents in some cultures commonly use corporal punishment, which means that they hit their kids. In the previous chapter, it was advised to gather information about a student before contacting the family about behavior problems. The reason is that the physical response at home may far outweigh what the school thinks is appropriate or necessary. A counselor, administrator, or ESOL teacher will have to tell a parent that, while they acknowledge the parental right to discipline their kids, in the United States it is against the law for parents to beat, deny food, or otherwise impose physical trauma on their children for any reason.

> *In one instance, a Southeast Asian mother was seen repeatedly banging her child on the back. The boy was generally a busy little guy, so he had had some behavior problems that his cousin-classmates told their shared babysitter, who told the parents. The little boy told his teacher that his back hurt, but it was because he had a cold. When the appropriate services called the mother, she said that it was their traditional way of treating a cough. The mother followed up with an angry note to school the next day saying that she didn't want to hear any more about it, ever. The school remained unsure, but, going forward, kept a closer eye on the student and managed his behavior without any phone calls home.*

4. Eye contact is a tough one for some kids. American teachers say over and over, "Look at me when I'm talking to you!" In many cultures, it is the depth of rudeness and disrespect for a child to look an adult in the eye, especially when they think they're in trouble.

5. American hand gestures are also easily misinterpreted. The American signal for "OK"—making a circle with the thumb and forefinger—is grossly obscene in Southern Europe and South America, particularly Brazil. In Asian countries, people often point or indicate position by using the middle finger, very different from American use.

   "Thumbs up" is crude and rude in the Middle East. Likewise obscene in Great Britain and Australia is the pointer and middle finger held up in a "V" for the number two, when held with the palm facing inward. The American method of signaling "come here" by crooking the index finger is used only for dogs in the Philippines. In Buddhist cultures, it is taboo to touch the top of a child's head, and to Middle Easterners, it is rude to show the bottom of the foot.

   This website illustrates some of the American hand gestures that are unintentionally insulting to other cultures: https://socialmettle.com/hand-gestures-in-different-cultures.

6. Some cultures deliberate by committee rather than individually; any decision affecting the group is made by consensus of the adults who have power in the immediate and extended family.

   Teachers see this in the high level of interaction within these groups. Some folks overeat, some oversleep, these kids overchat. They are almost always in groups, always talking, and are the last bunch to settle down and get quiet in class. And if they do, it doesn't last long. They want to do their work together. They are invested in minding everybody's business and enforcing their rules of fairness. For teachers, this is a squabbling pain in the neck, a huge distraction, and a hard nut to crack. "Take care of your own business" translates to "Everything is my business." "Do your own work" means "I'm just helping!"

7. Many cultures and religions have food restrictions that the school will need to know about when planning treats or parties. Some religious groups and vegetarians may not eat anything made with gelatin, as gelatin contains beef and pork. Dietary parameters should be taken as seriously as food allergies and treated accordingly. Some children just don't like American snack foods because they are too sweet.

GENDER AND EXPECTATIONS

Everybody wants their kids to do well at school, both academically and socially, and all parties are invested in that goal. Not everyone, though, understands "well" in the same way.

High Pressure

Some cultures put so much emphasis on school success that school staff can see the pressure those kids carry all day, every day. The child is viewed as a student, and as those NASA Apollo guys say, "Failure is not an option." They are fearful that their best isn't good enough, that they will embarrass their families by not being at the top of the heap, and that family aspirations will suffer at their little hands.

Sometimes they can't work at all over worry that they will make mistakes. These kids are often scheduled to within an inch of their young lives in tutoring, music lessons, and Saturday classes in family culture and language. They often have had all kinds of freedom as babies, until they reach school age and become students. Gender roles at school are less defined, but the go-to hierarchy favors boys, especially in cultures from India, the Middle East, Sudan, and Peru.

Low Pressure

Some cultures put less emphasis on academic success in favor of who the child is as a personification of their country, family, and gender. Boys are often pomaded, perfumed, and powdered, and, concerned about saving face, are "manly" and ready to defend their turf. Boys from certain countries take a stand when it's not necessary and frequently have an accusatory point of view; if something unwelcome happens, it's because somebody did something to them and, whoever it is, they're going to get it. Their goal is to grow up, get a job, and become a family protector. They operate in defense mode, fight over flight.

The following exchange was at a middle school at a beginning-of-the-year meeting between the principal and the ESOL teacher hired to set up a new ESOL program in the building.

Principal: Last year we had only eleven out-of-school suspensions for fighting.

ESOL teacher: Were those eleven suspensions mostly the same kids?

Principal: Yes. Three boys.

ESOL teacher: Would they all be ESOL students?

Principal: Yes.

ESOL teacher: Were they all from the same country?

Principal: Yes.

ESOL teacher: El Salvador?

Principal: Yes. I'd like you to prepare an in-service, please.

Boys may also hold a dim view of female teachers. One young Korean boy, the oldest child in his family, showed disrespect that warranted a parent conference. When the father came in, he wasted no time telling her, "You are a woman. I speak only to Mr. U. (the principal)." Sometimes passing that attitude up the line is the best idea. Just meeting the parent, though, makes a lot of the kid pieces click into place.

For girls, observed in elementary school as very often from Central American cultures, the emphasis may be more on appearance and status as helper. They come to school with curls, sparkles, and ruffles. They are nice little girls and they smell good, too. They are ready to sort or clean or help, but not always ready to do their school work. If there is more than one bedazzled little girl in a group, there could be a breakout of the Princess Wars. The teacher will have to intervene on who's ahead of whom in the line, who gets to sit closer to the teacher, whose turn it is, whose crayon is pinker. Their goals are more domestic. In one first-grade class, a little girl told her teacher that she had to put all her "juwry" (jewelry) on one arm because she burned the other arm ironing her big brother's shirt.

SOCIALIZING

As noted in chapter 1, many ESOL families live as close to their home cultures as they can. It affords a level of familiarity and comfort, but it can also limit how well their children integrate into the new culture.

First-generation EL kids don't have many, if any, playdates outside their family or church circles. Limited finances can mean that they don't attend sport or cultural events, don't travel except to visit their relatives, limit vacations to an overnight camping trip or a day at an amusement park, and generally have far fewer background experiences than non-EL students. In these cases, the teacher may have to encourage in-school friendships between certain classmates and build in background knowledge for instruction.

First-generation, and often second-generation, parents can be stuck in low-paying jobs. Lack of money has significant repercussions on the lives of their families. For a better idea of how severe financial need affect kids, consult *A Framework for Understanding Poverty* by Dr. Ruby Payne (https://www.ahaprocess. com/who-we-are/dr-ruby-payne/).

HOLIDAYS

First-generation ESOL students have a limited grasp of American holidays, just as American schools have a limited grasp of international holidays.

American Celebrations

Elementary classroom teachers usually do some fun and creative activities with their kids around special calendar dates. It helps the ESOLers if the teacher gives them some background, as well as the pertinent vocabulary for these events. Explain why some kids trick-or-treat (but remember that many religions and cultures don't allow it). Cover the basics of the First Thanksgiving and what it means to us now, broaden the approach to Christmas, Hanukkah, Kwanzaa, or other winter holidays with discussions about gift-giving and symbols.

Other events and holidays should be covered, too—New Years' Eve, Presidents' Day, Valentine's Day, St. Patrick's Day, Easter, Mother's Day, Father's Day, Fourth of July—whichever are appropriate to your group. Most elementary school libraries have nice books with good information about what and how Americans celebrate. Look for *American Holidays: Exploring Traditions, Customs, and Backgrounds* by Barbara Klebenow and Sara Fisher or *Celebration: The Story of American Holidays* by Lucille Recht Penner. Other books are grouped by the name of the particular holiday or celebration.

International Celebrations

This is a wonderful bonus! Some children celebrate exquisite and interesting holidays. It behooves the teacher to encourage all students to share what they're willing to, and for the teacher to provide some information, too. Sometimes a holiday is a holy day that entails excused absences, special clothing, food and/or fasting, jewelry, or skin painting. In schools with a range of nations in the community, there are great possibilities for an International Day or class project about home countries. EL kids doing big projects often are unable to do them at home, so need lots of supplies and support at school from the classroom teacher, para-educators, volunteers, and/or the ESOL teacher.

RESOURCES

An online hub for ESOL information is *Dave's ESL Café*, which has links to general holiday information, a holiday calendar, and activities by month.

Find Dave's ESL Café at http://eslcafe.com. Find information about a plethora of important American and international days at http://www.holidays.net/dates.htm.

KEY TAKEAWAYS

- First- and second-generation ESOL students are making transitions and straddling cultures.
- There is far more to an EL student than what is obvious at school—see the iceberg model.

- Home culture dictates much of the social and learning behaviors that schools see in first- and second-generation ELs (http://guide.culturecrossing.net/basics_business_student.php?id=11).
- EL parents want the best, and are doing their best, for their children.
- Holidays are a great way to help ELs learn about American customs and for them to share their home customs.

THREE

Domains, Testing, and Levels of English Language Learning

LANGUAGE DOMAINS

There are four major areas of language acquisition referred to as *domains*. The basics are, in order of ease of learning and typical mastery:

1. Listening – how well a student attends to and understands what he or she hears
2. Speaking – how clear, correct, and understandable a student is when talking
3. Reading – how well a student identifies, reads, and understands print
4. Writing – how clearly and correctly a student uses words "on paper"

The domains are usually broken down into subcategories of academic content areas—language arts, math, social studies, and science.

LISTENING

As noted in chapter 1, kids in the Silent Stage are listening. Listeners silently store and manipulate the language that they hear. They are working in the domain that is the most accessible and passive, but that is the foundation for skills in the other domains. It may look like they are not paying attention, but unless there's a problem with their ears, they're hearing something in English. If they're zoned out or tired from the effort, their ears are still awake at some level.

SPEAKING

The speaking domain involves how intelligible a student is. Its main components are articulation, grammar, vocabulary, and rate of speech. Different languages produce different numbers of syllables per minute, and it can be hard for some ELs to slow down or speed up. One grandmother from Spain, a regular volunteer at a local elementary school, was married to a native English speaker, had children and grandchildren who were native English speakers, and had been living in the United States for over thirty years. She was absolutely convinced that she was a fluent English speaker, but spoke so fast that even watching her mouth didn't help much. Throw in a lot of pure Castilian sibilant "s" sounds and the mind reeled.

Students who start to learn correct English pronunciation before the age of six have a better chance of learning the discrete sounds of English and are less likely in the long run to have accents. The muscles used to form sounds are different for different languages. Like other muscles, the more they are used, the more they develop, and the less they are used, the more they atrophy. Young language learners still have flexibility in their speech muscles. The sounds of "r" and "s" and "th" won't stymie them quite as much as they would older ELs. This isn't always a natural skill for ELs, so staff has to teach and practice specific sounds with them.

READING

Reading is considered a receptive or passive skill because the student is using language but not producing it. Passive doesn't mean easy, though. Young EL students in a language-rich elementary classroom are usually present for instruction in reading basics. They may or may not understand it all, but will likely take in as much as they can.

Young ELs are part of the reading-skills learning stream so are able to practice concepts of print, letter, sound, and word identification. Older ELs who come in after the learning-to-read instruction find themselves in the reading-to-learn stage and can be at a disadvantage without the basics of English. As noted earlier, students with high literacy at home will have an easier time with literacy in school. Older kids might get good at word-calling and recognize or figure out most of the print they see. Unless they understand what the words mean, though, they are not really reading.

Students whose L1 alphabets are different from English need more time to learn how to recognize, name, draw, and pronounce each new letter and typical letter combination before they can learn to read accurately and fluently in English. The Omniglot websites below name and show the world's alphabets. (Kazakhstan is in the process of switching to the Latin alphabet.)

- http://omniglot.com/writing/alphabets.htm
- http://omniglot.com/writing/syllabic.htm
- http://omniglot.com/writing/semanto-phonetic.php
- http://omniglot.com/writing/direction.htm

WRITING

The writing domain is often the hardest and the last for ELs to master. There's a lot for them to remember when trying to get written language out there. Native English speakers may also have trouble with writing, but they have the advantage of automaticity that nonnative speakers don't. ELs have to ask themselves:

- What do all the words in the question/prompt mean?
- What does it want me to do?
- What words do I need?
- How do I spell all of the words for the answer?
- How do I draw some of those letters?
- What order do the words go in?
- Where do the capital letters go?
- What punctuation do I need?
- Where does the punctuation go?
- How long does this have to be?

By the time they run through it all, at speeds that vary per student, it's very possible that they've lost track of what they're supposed to do.

The domains do not progress equally nor at the same pace, but they are usually reasonably staggered. A strong ESOL student can sometimes cross the English proficiency finish line in as little as one to two years. True mastery of academic language in all domains, though, most often takes five to ten years. English is hard. It takes a long time to learn it well.

TESTING ENGLISH LANGUAGE PROFICIENCY

By federal law, every student identified as an English Learner has to take an English proficiency assessment each year to determine if they have made consistent progress. Different states use different assessment tools, but they all must record scores in the four domains. The content area subcategories are usually embedded in each domain section of the test. An overview of federal laws about identifying and providing instruction for ELLs can be found at this joint Department of Education and Department of Justice website: https://www2.ed.gov/about/offices/list/ocr/docs/dcl-factsheet-el-students-201501.pdf.

No student may take the assessment more than once a year. If a student is absent during ESOL testing and does not return before the state-mandated testing window closes, that student's scores from the previous year carry forward. A boy whose family regularly returned to the home country for an extended stay missed ESOL testing two years in a row. He was an excellent EL student who made steady progress in all domains and was very nearly fluent within three years. But because the school had no formal testing reports for him during those years, "Why is this kid stagnant?!" thudded from the state through levels of administration to the teacher of record. His absences were documented and recorded in his cume and ESOL folders, along with work samples and informal assessments, so neither the local program nor the ESOL teacher were in jeopardy. This is a good illustration of the value of clear and current school records for ELLs.

ESOL students arrive in schools at all points of the year. If an ESOL student registers in a school at any time during the formal assessment timeframe, that student must take the test. There have been instances when a kid shows up one morning, on the last or second to last day of testing, and must immediately take as many parts of the assessment as possible. If the school can't get it all in, the ESOL or school test coordinator has to document why.

Federal and state funding for language-acquisition programs is closely tied to how well schools and districts move their ELs through the language-acquisition program, based on the results of the annual test. States set annual progress goals for each school and district based on:

- the percentage of ELs who move up from level to level,
- the percentage of ELs who "exit" the ESOL program, and
- the percentage of ELs who show proficiency with content vocabulary.

LEVELS OF ENGLISH LANGUAGE PROFICIENCY

Districts use different terms to name and describe the levels of English Language Proficiency. They're often based on the terms their assessment uses, but fit generally within Newcomer (pre-Beginner), Beginner, Intermediate, and Advanced, with low and high bands per level. Districts often use the levels to provide guidelines for how much direct ESOL instruction the student should receive per week.

Newcomer

Newcomer/pre-Beginner is something of a stand-alone level, as it means no or almost no English Language skills. A newcomer is a student who is brand new to the country. Newcomers need consistent support from their teachers in adapting to the new culture. The school will have to be present for social-emotional help as well as for getting the Newcomer into the academic stream (remember Anastasia in chapter 1?) The book *The Newcomer Student: An Educator's Guide to Aid Transition* by Louise H. Kreuzer is a valuable tool in these situations.

Newcomers will probably not be able to respond to any instructions or questions given in English. They will need immediate help finding and identifying school staff, the bathroom, school locations, and classroom supplies. They may be worried about lunch and dismissal, especially if they are to ride a bus.

If the teacher has had time to let the class know that a new student is coming, the kids will have a chance to talk about times when they were new or confused or scared at school. It will make getting and staying settled in the classroom go more smoothly if there are a few kids that the teacher can assign as buddies for the Newcomer. Newcomers will usually watch their classmates for cues of what to do.

Newcomers may or may not have had schooling in their home countries. For kids in the lower grades, missed education is a little less cumbersome than it is for those who come in past the elementary years. Most school systems have special programs for middle- or high-school students whose education was interrupted for more than a year, or whose school history is inconsistent.

Teachers may have to help Newcomers get used to things at school that most kids take for granted:

- English
- sitting at a desk or table
- working alone and/or quietly
- working in a group or cooperatively
- walking in line
- raising their hands
- school schedules
- school personnel and their jobs
- safety drills

In 1978 and 1979, when they were first arriving in numbers, students from Vietnam were amazed by the amount of food on a school lunch tray and that each child got their own. That was far easier than fire drills, as their response to loud sirens was to take cover. It was hard to clear the building with kids huddled under their desks or in the closets.

The US Department of Education compiled a brochure about the many facets of Newcomers and how schools can help. A "Newcomer Toolkit" can be found at https://www2.ed.gov/about/offices/list/oela/ newcomers-toolkit/ncomertoolkit.pdf.

Level 1–2 Beginner

A Level 1–2 student may or may not have been born in the United States. Those who were born in the United States may have had some exposure to social English. They are usually less confounded than Newcomers, but their expressive language may be just as limited.

Level 1–2 students are able to attend a little, follow some directions in class, and are often in the Listening stage. These students understand pictures or other visual representations of words, and can point, gesture, or otherwise indicate without speaking that they understand something. They can respond correctly to simple, short directions, yes/no questions, and some "wh" questions, especially if there has been some practice, support from visuals, demonstration, or sensory interaction. Adjustment behaviors are probably still in play.

When Level 1–2 ESOL students start speaking, it is often in short, one to two syllable utterances. They will use single nouns to name familiar objects, although they may mispronounce words so badly that the listener can't understand. They may be able to use a few verbs accurately, but again, with some significant pronunciation errors. Students at this level often drop or add word endings that teachers must drill with repetition for kids to internalize the correct ways to say them:

- haves—have, has
- doan—don't
- can—can and can't
- singular endings for plurals (no ending "s" sound)
- mines—mine
- witch—with

Other common mispronunciations are:

- d/f/s/t/v for th—baffroom for bathroom, bruvver / brudder - brother, duh - the
- dz for j—dzump for jump
- sh for s—yesh for yes
- sh for ch—share for chair, shocolate for chocolate
- es for s—estay for stay
- j or l for y—jello / lellow for yellow

- v for w—vee for we
- in' for ing—workin', eatin', playin'
- b for v—berry for very

Beginners who have some knowledge of the Latin alphabet may need to learn the English pronunciation of letter names. For instance, "ay" in English is the letter "a" but is "ah" in Spanish, "ee" in English is the letter "e", but in Spanish is the letter "i."

Reading for Beginning ESOL students sometimes starts with concepts of print, but always includes:

- identifying letters
- naming letters
- discerning upper and lower case letters
- ordering the letters of the alphabet
- practicing discrete sounds
- recognizing beginning sounds
- word shapes and environmental print (school signs)
- identifying beginning sight/high-frequency words
- reading beginning sight/high frequency words

Writing starts with the Beginner putting pencil to lined paper for the same skills listed above. For students coming in with experience in a non-Latin alphabet, it is a matter of first "drawing" the letters. Most Beginning writers start by tracing, then copying, letters while they name them. All early writers must learn:

- horizontal spacing between letters
- letters in the vertical space (the ones with tails—beware the flying g, j, p, q, y)
- spacing between words
- relative sizes of upper- and lowercase letters

Beginning ESOL writers can have the same confusions that native English early writers have in pre-K to grade 2 with mostly lower case letters like b/d, n/m, h/n, K/k and directionality for b, d, c, f, p, q, s, and z. In a class with large numbers of early writers, teachers may find themselves having to check the A-B-C chart to remind themselves which way the letters really go. Beginning writers who struggle with making certain sounds will subvocalize them incorrectly and write accordingly.

Beginning EL readers and writers can do the following:

- understand and use labels
- use letter–sound knowledge to produce semiaccurate spellings
- recognize word patterns
- use word banks
- fill in the blanks with sentence starters
- interpret graphic organizers

They rely heavily on cues, modeling, pictures or other visuals, and prompting via leading questions or beginning sounds. Their message is not always clear, but their uses of letters and words approach American English conventions.

Level 3–4 Intermediate

There is a school of thought that, at this level, presenting material to ELLs in their home language helps them build English skills. This includes using L1 to communicate with parents or guardians. Whatever their merits, those instructional ideas are not part of the discussion here for several reasons, largely based on one of the Lessons Learned, "never assume."

- Most students in elementary grades have not had sufficient instruction in L1 to use it in correctly learning English across all domains.
- Many parents/family members have limited literacy in L1.

- There are hundreds of non-English languages at play. Who will provide all those translations and L1 materials for every grade, in all content areas, at every ESOL level?
- American schools are de-facto immersion programs, with English as the target language.

There is certainly a place for bilingual education, but within its own formalized structure. If our goal at this early stage in general education is to produce learners who will eventually participate in and contribute to their English-speaking communities, then our focus must be on English. Homes that have the means to maintain facility and/or literacy in the first language will do so, and the connections to English will establish themselves. American schools must proceed, however, without assuming that most students have home literacy or language experiences to support development of functional, correct English language skills.

Intermediate ELs can use some content-specific vocabulary and have improved receptive skills. This makes it easier for them to pay attention and to follow directions, although they still need extra time to process and translate incoming messages. At this stage, negative behaviors associated with language confusion or limited acculturation should be subsiding.

Intermediate Listening skills include:

- sequencing from oral directions
- following modeled, multistep directions
- classifying from oral directions
- finding details, objects, and pictures based on oral descriptions

Intermediate listeners will likely still watch their classmates for cues and may need repetition of directions and descriptions. They may still feel insecure about their work, so might be slow to start or finish. Whenever possible, it helps them to make cognitive leaps and connections if there are visual models to attach to their listening. Models can be anything from gestures and pictures to written words. As with Beginning students, it's important for speakers to articulate carefully and to modify their rate of speech.

Some languages phrase questions differently, and requests are made simply by a change of inflection. Teachers may hear, "I can drink the water?" It bears emphasizing that this can be steadily, if not readily, improved by having kids repeat the teacher's correction, *"May I please have/get a drink of water?"* before the kid ambles off on the scenic route to the drinking fountain. The same is true for bathroom breaks, although sometimes it's best to worry about conventions later and just let them rush out.

Native English speakers use "reductions" that can make it hard for Beginning and Intermediate Listeners to grasp what is being said. A reduction is something of a multi-word contraction that most native English speakers hear and understand very easily, but that are not as easily interpreted by ELs. Here are some common American English reductions:

- j'eat—did you eat
- mornin'—good morning
- "uh" for "to + infinitive"

    - needuh—need to
    - haftuh—have to
    - wannuh—want to
    - gunnuh—going to
    - usetuh—used to
    - ummunnuh—I'm going to
    - postuh—supposed to

- c'mon—come on
- arnchuh—aren't you
- cuz—because
- uhlottuh—a lot of
- d'jya—did you (Where'd'jya go after lunch? How'd'jya do on your test?)
- "uh" for "al"—uhright for alright, uhready for already, uhmost for almost
- supponuh—explained in this exchange:

Student: *How do you spell "supponuh?"*
Teacher: *I don't know that word. Tell me the sentence you need it for.*
Student: *You know, like in "One supponuh time."*

Folks talking to ELs at this stage must consistently pronounce each word distinctly so ELs can discern them as separate units and then say, read, and write them correctly. The mispronunciations of Beginning levels may persist.

Small words can make big problems; prepositions, prepositional phrases, and pronouns can trip kids up and usually need specific and repeated instruction, correction, and practice. Many American English prepositions and prepositional phrases are idiomatic and just have to be memorized. "On" is a good example:

- Turn the light on.
- On your mark . . .
- Put your shoes on.
- What's on TV?
- What's going on?
- On time (not to be confused with "in time")
- On the way
- Come on
- On Tuesday
- On my birthday

(Note that some kids say, "On tomorrow" or "On yesterday," which needs to be consistently corrected.)

It's not unusual for an Intermediate EL to throw any available preposition at a sentence and hope it sticks. That certainly would be easier and plays well into the unclearly-delivered-but-comprehensible profile of Intermediate ESOL students. But, as always, it disrupts language flow and accuracy down the line.

The concept of pronouns is not confounding, but using them correctly in their subject, object, and possessive roles can be. After direct instruction, hearing them used well in context, along with continued practice, usually clears things up over time.

In an Intermediate reading group with first-grade ESOLers, Miss Rogers was doing a picture-walk of The Little Red Hen. *The cover illustration showed the hard-working hen sweeping her front porch, while a pile of lazy farmyard friends flops against the side of the house. When asked, "What is the Little Red Hen doing?" the happy answer came back from one student, "He broomin' she house!"*

This is correct in the incorrect, Intermediate ESOL kind of way. There are lots of teachable language moments in that little scenario, and we'll cover these in a later chapter. For our purposes here, the teacher said, "Yes! *She* is sweeping *her* house. Good job!"

Intermediate ESOLers make a variety of generalizations as they internalize the rules of their new language. They put "ed" at the end of many verbs to make past tense—sleeped, eated, bringed—and add "s" to the end of possessive pronouns—"mines" for "mine"—and create compound words.

An Intermediate second-grader had two speeds: slow and slower. No matter how much lead time she had, she was always last. One morning as her group was leaving Miss Rogers's room, they lined up and waited for her (again) at the door. She looked pretty grumpy as she put her things away, so Miss Rogers asked, "Are you okay, Merari?"

"No. Why I always gotta be the line backer?"

Here's another exchange with an ESOL student in Kindergarten:

Teacher: What did you do yesterday, Elena?

Elena: We goed to the Medicine Bank (the pharmacy).

As ear-grating or entertaining as they may be to the teacher, errors serve the students well as they help make kids more willing to:

- retell stories
- describe feelings
- predict
- ask questions
- explain their basic thought processes
- participate in class discussions

The aforementioned skills play into reading and writing. Students will say as they hear, and write as they say. Garbled is as garbled does. Intermediate EL students can:

- answer prompts about personal connections to what they are reading
- match titles or captions to pictures
- tell about story structure in fiction
- recognize a consistently growing list of words
- follow a reading passage
- find information or answer questions based on the text
- express learning from illustrations

With modeling and guidance, they can further transfer their skills to writing.

Intermediate writers understand most of the writing process, including prewriting, and it helps them pull away from the "one-and-done" mindset, which can result in a "let's get this over with" delivery. Because of all the cogs in the writing wheel that take a long time to master, it serves ESOL students better to be guided many times through the steps of direct skill instruction—prewriting, revising, editing, and re-teaching—as errors come up.

Most language learners find it easier to put pencil to paper if they are able to write about personal experiences and the teacher's focus is on just one part of the writing—a particular convention, use of target vocabulary, an accurate response to a question, and so forth. Technology can often make kids more productive in writing, but the multimodal use of pencil and paper helps build and retain skills.

A very small third-grade boy named Li held the all-time ESOL record for Last Kid to Start Writing. This articulate, very smart little guy was a-tremble about lots of stuff, but writing seemed to be at the top of his Things to Avoid list. Early in the year, for a class assignment to write a short, scaffolded letter to a Special Olympics athlete, his paper steadfastly remained blank. Miss Rogers took him aside for a little coaching pep talk.

Miss Rogers: What sports do you like?

Li: I. don't. like. any. sports.

Miss Rogers: What do you do on the playground?

Li: I watch the other kids.

Miss Rogers: Do you play with the other kids?

Li: No. They are all bigger than me and I would get clobbered.

Miss Rogers (thinking, "If you can use the word 'clobbered,' why are you in ESOL?"—a question for proficiency testing time): I understand. Then just write one sentence that says "congratulations" and one that says "good luck." Use the words on the board to start. Do you want some help?

Li: OK. I don't need help.

So that's what he did because his experience with physical activity didn't warrant or provide more than the minimum. It also helped Miss Rogers think of better ways to reach him and his equally reticent twin. In a later assignment, each was able to detail in great length the thrill of being "ring barriers" in a family wedding, and the injustice of their father not letting them carry their tablets.

The Intermediate EL student delivers a clear message most of the time, despite generalized errors. Intermediate ESOLers will respond to correction and may even be able to self-correct. An independent English language user is on the way!

Level 5–6 Advanced/Exited

Advanced ESOL students usually feel good about themselves academically. They most often have multilingual friends and work partners, and can express their learning in almost every academic arena with little or no support (except maybe writing). They can recognize and correct language errors, keep up with the class, work independently, contribute to a group, and flex their intellectual muscles. They often state English as their preference, sometimes to their families' unhappiness.

For students who have come to English beyond the age of two, this is a typical transfer of language power, and a goal reached. Families may express regret that their student is losing part of their culture. Unless the family as a whole has given up the first language, though, it will remain intact in the student in whatever ways the family requires them to use it. For Advanced ESOLers in school, it's very important for their school success that they be allowed to use their English skills as they will.

In Listening, Level 5–6 ESOL students are able to:

- follow complex, multistep oral directions which include grade-level content vocabulary
- understand literal and figurative language, as well as some humor, sarcasm, and idioms
- attend to sentence structures of different lengths
- understand like ideas presented in multiple ways
- retrieve what they have previously heard and connect it to new material

Given the availability of technology-based audiovisual presentations, the opportunities are great for these ELs to expand their learning and to show it creatively. Those combinations and opportunities at the right not-too-frustrating levels almost always help language learners hold their ground or move ahead.

Students who are ready to exit ESOL services speak clearly in a variety of sentence lengths with vocabulary that is equal to what their classmates use. They can:

- verbally defend an answer
- make a judgment or application using language to express connections
- understand multistep directions
- give a series of directions academically as well as socially (as in game rules)
- completely take part in hands-on experiences and recount the processes
- describe the details of personal experiences and connect them to other students' stories or to school

In reading, these students are comfortable with grade-level text and can:

- understand and use both explicit and implied language
- summarize what they have read in both fiction and nonfiction without a blizzard of unnecessary detail
- recognize, understand, and correctly use idioms and other figurative language

Advanced students are often independent readers, interested in picking their own topics in their genre/s of choice. Not every capable reader in ESOL loves it, but they can read and understand what passages mean.

Writing may remain a somewhat clunky endeavor for even Advanced ELs, given all the aforementioned cogs in the big moving wheel of composition. A Level 5–6 ESOLer, however, will make fewer errors and those will often be consistent, founded in the same misunderstanding, rather than a variety of mistakes based on a collection of unstable, poorly used information. Nonetheless, these students will generally be able to:

- write complex sentences with mostly accurate mechanics and appropriate vocabulary spelled correctly
- write original works or summaries
- combine research from multiple sources with content words into original sentences to answer prompts, or in grade-level reports and projects

Writing can still be a time-consuming and tiring process, so even an Advanced EL writer will sometimes cave in and write an answer by simply copying something with a nice collection of key words that they need. It's easy to recognize that particular strategy, so a follow-up question of "What does this word/ phrase/sentence mean?" may warrant a rewrite. In all cases, if kids write something they can't explain, they have to change it to something they can.

All academic fields being otherwise fairly level, Advanced ESOL students are quite independent and holding their own on grade-level work. Students at this level may still need a few accommodations, based on scores in all the domains and input from their teachers.

BEGINNING LEVEL PROFICIENCY GOALS

- Follow typical short, oral classroom directions
- Talk in basic social interactions
- Answer short yes/no questions in simple present tense about familiar subjects
- Use simple present tense to speak short answers about familiar subjects
- Ask simple questions using a language formula (Is it . . . ? What is . . . ?)
- Ask permission with formulaic language (May I please . . . ?)
- State basic needs using formulaic structure (I need . . .)
- Answer simple present-tense "wh" questions about a familiar subject
- Use simple present tense to ask and answer "How many?" questions
- Use simple present tense to make affirmative and negative statements about familiar subjects
- Use simple present tense of "be" and "have" to make affirmative and negative statements about familiar subjects
- Use "can" and "can't" in simple statements
- Use present continuous tense in statements and questions
- Ask and answer in future tense using the word "will"
- Use simple future-tense statements in statements of intent, cause-effect, and predictions
- Use demonstrative pronouns (this, that, these, those)
- Use subject pronouns correctly
- Use "and" to combine nouns in simple sentences (Pete and Ellen can swim. I like cats and kittens.)
- Correctly use singular and regular plural nouns
- Use articles "a" and "the" with nouns
- Use adjectives after "be" to describe basic attributes (It is red. They are small.)
- Understand and use basic prepositions of place (in, on, under, over, in front of, behind, on top of, next to, between)

NOTE: *Simple present tense* is used for events that happen regularly or repeatedly. "I ride the bus. You sit next to me." *Present progressive tense* at this level describes something that is happening right now. "I am riding the bus. You are sitting next to me."

INTERMEDIATE LEVEL PROFICIENCY GOALS

- Follow and give simple one- or two-step oral and written directions
- Use complete sentences to ask and answer simple past, present, and future "wh" questions
- Use complete sentences to ask and answer choice questions (Do you like to _____ or ____?)
- Use complete sentences to answer yes/no questions
- Ask and answer simple-tense questions of "why" and "how" about familiar subjects
- Use modal verbs to ask polite questions in simple tenses (May I please . . . ? Will you please . . . ?)
- Use correct subject-verb agreement in statements and questions
- Make affirmative and negative statements with "have" and "has"
- Use simple past tense to make continuous statements about personal experiences (I was watching TV when my sister came home.)
- Use high-frequency regular and irregular past-tense verbs (said, had, was, were, took, went, ate, saw, heard)
- Use "going to" to make future statements
- Use articles "a" and "an" with nouns
- Use regular and irregular plural nouns (children, women, men, teeth, feet, people)
- Use possessive pronouns my, our, your, his, her, their
- Use "know how to . . ." in affirmative and negative statements and questions about ability
- Use common conjunctions and transition words to summarize (and, but, then, because, so)
- Recognize and use common synonym and antonym pairs
- Use adjectives in correct word order with nouns (number, size, condition, color)
- Use sequencing words to describe procedures or events (first, next, then, last, finally, before, after)

NOTE: *Simple past*: walked, saw, learned; *Simple future*: will go, will remember, am going to see. *Past progressive*: was walking, were listening (when something else also happened); *Future progressive*: will be going to practice, will be singing in music class.

ADVANCED LEVEL PROFICIENCY GOALS

- Give and follow multistep oral and written directions for academic tasks
- Use complete sentences to ask and answer "wh" questions, including "Why?" and "How?"
- Use conditional statements and questions (grade 3 +) with the words "would" and "could"
- Ask and answer polite requests with modals "would," "could," and "should"
- Offer opinions or suggestions with modals "would," "could," and "should"
- Use modals in affirmative and negative statements of position or opinion (to persuade)
- Express probability using the modal "might"
- Respond to questions in the passive voice—How are your favorite cookies made?
- Make simple affirmative statements in the passive voice (grade 3 +)
- Use irregular past-tense verbs in statements and questions
- Use present perfect tense in telling about personal experiences (grade 3 +)—I have been there.
- Express past habitual events with "used to" (grade 3+)—We used to live in Guatemala.
- Use indirect object pronouns me, you, her, him, us, them
- Expand and use conjunctions and transition words in speaking and writing
- Explain reasons or purpose using *to + infinitive* or *for + verb/ing*—Water is used to wash. Water is used for washing.
- Use gerunds as nouns—Reading is my favorite hobby.
- Use quantifiers few, some, many, all, too, enough, plenty
- Use a/an/some/any with count and noncount nouns in statements and questions about needs or wants—She needs some scissors. They want some rest after school. I don't have any money.

NOTE: *Present perfect tense* is used to describe an event that happened at a nonspecific time in the past. It may not be used with a specific-time statement. Make present perfect with have/has + past participle of the verb: "*I have seen her before*" (not "*I have seen her yesterday*").

KEY TAKEAWAYS

- Adjustment is much more involved than language only.
- There are four domains of language learning: Listening, Speaking, Reading, and Writing.
- All identified ELLs must take their state's annual progress assessment to set their proficiency levels in the domains.
- The domains are measured across major academic areas.
- Progress in domains is usually staggered but fairly consistent.
- There are three basic levels of language acquisition, all with Low and High bands: Newcomer/ Beginning, Intermediate, and Advanced.
- Newcomer/Beginning students will have little or no comprehension and generally cannot make themselves understood in English.
- Intermediate students understand more than they can produce; their production may be inaccurate but the message is fairly clear.
- Advanced students understand and produce language with skill near or at that of native English speakers.
- Schools cannot fairly assume literacy or skills in the home language spoken at home.
- Reductions and mispronunciations transfer to student writing.

FOUR
How to Talk to Your ELLs

PACE YOURSELF

Most teachers had foreign language classes at some point between middle school and college. Most can remember their first weeks or months, struggling to understand what the instructor was saying at the appropriate syllables-per-minute in the target language, and then bit by bit learning to discern sounds that became understandable words that became clear messages. The same process happens with ELLs.

First, learn how to correctly pronounce each student's preferred name.

Receptive Language

School has a "hurry up" factor that can be troublesome for ELLs, and that teachers have to side-step in order to make the most of instructional time with ESOL students. They have to purposefully move out of their typical speech speed for a fluent-English audience, slow things down, and enunciate carefully so the not-English-fluent students can attend and pick up whatever sounds or words they recognize. It isn't necessary to sloth through every sentence of the day, but when talking to the ELLs, watch your speed and emphasize the nouns and verbs. Look at your ESOL students as you talk so they know that they are part of the message.

It also helps to slow down the message. ESOL students will grasp and remember more if pertinent information is delivered in chunks rather than in lumps. Teachers often give a string of oral directions that ESOL students can't follow but that are easy to change. For example, "Good morning, everyone. Take your things out of your backpacks, put your backpacks away, and then go to your seats to do your morning work."

It works just as well, and far more easily for ESOLers, if that message is delivered with brief pauses between sentences as, "Good morning. Get your papers and snacks out. Put your backpacks away. Go to your seats. Start your morning work." This is second nature for most early-elementary teachers and is especially important for kids just starting out in English. For young learners, it can be a best practice across the board. Keep your sentences short, with only one message per sentence. Pause, repeat, summarize, and check for understanding depending on how your students are responding. Many kids won't want to or know to ask about what they don't understand, but teachers can assume that there will be gaps.

Visually, this translates to having wider-than-normal spaces between words when writing for ELLs. The spaces make it easier for students to see word shapes, and to figure out discrete words and sounds. Skip a line and double space, when possible, for the same reasons. A crowd of words makes it hard for ELs to see and sort the parts.

Part of slowing down the message is repetition, another best practice in early grades. For early ELLs, say the same thing the same way with emphasis on nouns and verbs. For intermediate ELLs, it's okay to repeat or rephrase. Say it twice. Repeat yourself. Say it again.

Avoid text that looks long and crowded like this and that doesn't have breaks or any other kind of visual to interrupt the intimidating appearance of long words and sentences. Don't use skinny fonts.

Use text that gives kids a chance to see and interpret each word. Leave spaces to keep the words from looking too scary to try. Use wide fonts that makes letters the same way kids are taught to print. Century Gothic works well.

Figure 4.1.   Created by author.

Remembering one of the Lessons Learned from the Introduction, this is a place where teachers can't assume that all students have the background they need for the lesson. A preteaching activity that allows kids to talk about what they already know will give the teacher a chance to discern what's missing, and for the ELLs to get some of the supporting background and make some connections.

Teachers and classmates can fill in some small gaps, in general ways, but teachers should understand that many EL kids just haven't had exposure or practice with background information or skills that we take for granted with native-English elementary students. Allow repetition so ESOL students hear it more than once in different ways. Teachers can repeat what students say and add any details that will benefit the Limited English Proficient (LEP) kids. As new vocabulary comes up, it can be posted for future reference.

Productive Language

The pace for ELL productive language also takes pause. Give ESOL students some lead time and thinking time. Tell them what the class will talk about and that you want them to say something in the group.

Let's revisit *The Little Red Hen*, now that "he finish broomin' she house."

Beginner:

- *Look at this picture/any picture you want.* (Help find a picture if necessary.)
- *Tell me one word about the picture. You may point to it in the picture.*
- *Touch your nose when you are ready.* (Demonstrate.)

or

- *I want you to answer a question about the story.*
- *You may say "yes" or "no."*
- *This is the question: Did the other animals help the Little Red Hen?*
- *Touch your nose when you are ready.*

Intermediate:

- *Look at any picture you want.*
- *Tell me something about the picture.*
- *Tell me two words you can use to describe the picture.* (Help if needed.)
- *Touch your nose when you are ready.*

or

- *I will ask you a question.*
- *You have time to think about it.*
- *Here is the question: Why did the Little Red Hen keep all the bread?*
- *Touch your nose when you are ready.*

Advanced:

These students won't need the special pauses and short directions, but it will help them make their thinking and answers more fluent if they have a general heads-up.

- *We will talk about how different characters acted in the story. Think about one time when you needed help, and one time when you helped somebody else.*
- *Tell me how that is like part of the story.*

or

- *Are you like the Little Red Hen or the other animals? Tell me why you think so.*
- *Who do you know that is like the Little Red Hen? Why do you think so?*
- *Who do you know that is like the other animals? Why do you think so?*

The next examples are about the very early chapter book, *Mr. Putter and Tabby Pour the Tea* by Cynthia Rylant. This is part of a K–2 series, much like Rylant's equally usable *Henry and Mudge* stories. If these are too simple, *Because of Winn Dixie* by Kate DiCamillo is excellent for grades 2–4. All of these books focus on loving owner–pet friendships.

Beginner:

- *I want you to answer a question . . .*
- *This is the question: Did the cat like her new house?*
- *Look at me and touch your nose when you are ready.* (Demonstrate.)

Pictures also work. Show or give the student a picture or illustration, and say,

- *I want you to say one word about this picture.*
- *Touch your nose when you are ready.*

It's okay for them to get help from a buddy and for the teacher to prompt with beginning sounds, key words, or a sentence starter. If there isn't a nose-touch, check with the student and try again later if necessary.

Intermediate:

These kids won't need such a specific lead-in, but they will need the think-time.

- *Today we will talk about the old cat and the man who took her home.*
- *I want you to tell me one thing that the cat did at her new house.*
- *Touch your nose when you are ready.*

It's OK to prompt intermediate kids.

Advanced:

Advanced kids may need some time to recollect vocabulary, but they can keep pace with the discussion speed of the general group. It's okay to prompt Advanced students with clues, beginning sounds, or sentence starters, but they probably won't need help.

At any level, if the student is uncomfortable or gets stuck, say, *"Do you want to tell me later?"* or *"Do you want to think some more?"* or *"Do you want some help?"* There are usually volunteers more than willing to help. It's fine to pull a student aside to let him or her respond without a class audience. The objective is to get students to use some English, not to put the spotlight on them.

The pause is important to ELLs. There are a lot of time-consuming language conversions going on in their heads, and the well-placed pause gives them a chance to catch up a bit. Typical wait time in classroom discourse is three or four seconds. ELLs need seven to ten seconds. When they get to the productive language stage, pauses will still be important, as kids will need time to think about the question, find the words and structures they need for the answer, practice it internally, and then actually say what they want to say.

THIS IS TENSE. KEEP IT SIMPLE.

English verbs carry a lot of weight. They make the most structural changes for different uses and impart the how and when of the sentence. They are complicated for ELs. To clear that cluttered verb trail, stick with simple tenses at the beginning. Start with simple present and then move into simple past and simple future.

- Simple present—something that happens regularly or often. *We play outside after school.*
- Simple past—something that happened and ended in the past. *We played outside after school.*
- Simple future—something that will happen and end later. *We will play after school.*

Intermediate and Advanced ESOL students can understand and use progressive/continuous tenses, in which the main verb has an "ing" ending and needs an auxiliary/helping verb in front of it. Many ELLs have trouble remembering to use the auxiliary verb and to fully pronounce the "ing" ending. Teachers must correct and recorrect and re-recorrect this, and have students restate properly until they can self-correct, it becomes second-nature, and it can transfer to accurate writing. Students absolutely must move away from "We learnin'" to "We are learning." The auxiliary is the appropriate tense and form of "to be."

- Present progressive with am, are, is—a continuing action, happening now. *We are reading about pets.*
- Past progressive with was, were—an unfinished action from the past. *We were reading about pets.*
- Future progressive with will be *or* going to + infinitive—a future action that will take some time. *We will be reading about pets. We are going to read about pets.*

BE AN ACTIVE *ACTIVE* SPEAKER

The first "active" here means active voice. Structure the words so that the subject is doing the action, instead of an action happening to the subject. Passive voice complicates the verb tenses. It moves the "what is this about" noun to a distant place near the end of the sentence and makes it hard for ELLs to find. To keep the message simple and clear, especially for Beginning and most Intermediate ELLs, use active voice as much as possible.

Some examples:

- *Do your work.* (not *Get your work done.*)
- *Tell your grown-ups about it.* (not *Your grown-ups need to be told about it.*)
- *Explain the answer.* (not *The answer has to be explained.*)

For this group of learners, stick to a simple subject-predicate/noun-verb structure as much as possible.

The other "active" means to move with the language. ELLs glean a lot of information from facial expressions, gestures, movements, body language, and any non-language-based way to infuse meaning into the message. It can feel silly and overdone, but using your face and body to support what you are saying helps these students make connections to the words and their meanings. This strategy links nicely to synonyms, adjectives, adverbs, and inference in illustrations and reading, and authors' word choices in writing. It can be a lot of fun to have students provide words according to the face and body actions of someone else, or to do their own demonstrations based on words the teacher provides.

Try this with students. Use body language with facial expressions, and throw in some tone of voice, with the simple phrase *"come here"*:

- Cross your arms, make angry eyes, and speak with a hiss, *"Come here."*
- Put your finger to your lips and whisper, *"Come here."*
- Open your arms in a hug-like movement, put an "aww" in your voice, and say, *"Come here."*

- Shake your fists next to your head, clench your teeth, lower your voice, and say, *"Come here."*

Same words, but with different actions, different tones, and different meanings. Talk with your students about how they know the feeling of each example and, for non-Beginners, what feeling it showed for the speaker. Have kids indicate with thumbs up or down if each message is positive or negative, and let them provide words for the teacher or students to post for the group. As your speakers become readers, pull your examples from the reading material. In your read-alouds, do the voices, expressions, and gestures that impart or support the meaning of the words.

For higher Intermediate and for Advanced students, when kids are ready for synonyms, do the same kind of activity, substituting words for "said" or "walked" or "went." Have kids demonstrate and say what each action tells about the person doing it.

- *She tiptoed out of the room.* (She is scared or sneaky.)
- *She jumped out of the room.* (She is excited.)
- *She shuffled out of the room.* (She feels sad.)
- *She stamped out of the room.* (She's mad.)
- *He yelled, "No!"* (He is mad or scared.)
- *He asked, "No?"* (He feels confused or unsure.)
- *He whispered, "No."* (He is scared, tired, disappointed.)
- *He mumbled, "No."* (He feels mad or discouraged or doesn't want to talk.)

MORE THAN WORDS

Visuals and hands-on items are a great help to ELLs, and there are lots of good resources. For best effect, use what is known in the ESOL world as "realia." Realia means objects or activities related to real life. You can't always bring realia to the classroom, but if you can, it's a proven way to help ESOL students develop understanding. Realia for objects is usually the real thing—real fossils, real tools, real artifacts. Realia for activities is in the doing. If you have space to move around, move around.

Representations also offer good support for ELs. Models or photographs of real items help establish the links between items or actions and words. For younger students, toys can be used as models. Animal figures, doll/play houses with people and furniture, play food/kitchen items, transportation toys, and other hands-on things help students learn and remember which words go with items or actions.

Teachers of young students know to build in the distracting "play" factor. Kids have time to handle items and get some informal play-learning out of their systems before those items become tools of formal learning. Good timing helps, too. Get the items in front of the ELs before the topic is presented for instruction so they have familiarity with the vocabulary. Almost every kid in the room will want to be hands-on, with the advantage to ESOL students that they will be having fun and interacting naturally with English-speaking classmates.

Illustrations are almost always available to help ELLs. The media specialist or school librarian can help teachers as well as ESOL students find print materials with the needed illustrations and other text features. Look for pictures that represent a variety of cultures and ethnicities, especially the groups in your class.

If there is an ESOL specialist for the building, he or she may have materials that match grade-level objectives. There are a number of illustrated picture dictionaries geared to many levels of English learning that can give ESOL students a lot of information with minimal language. Two of the most widely used sets of picture dictionaries are published by Oxford University Press and Longman.

Other helpful visuals include timelines, graphs, charts, or organizers appropriate to the grade level.

I DON'T GET IT

ELLs need language delivered to them clearly and cleanly. In Beginning and Intermediate levels, they do not usually understand American sarcasm, negative statements, or idioms. Sarcasm is, in effect, saying the opposite of what you mean and is a bad language example. In addition, certain tones of voice that accompany American humor or sarcasm may be offensive or hurtful in ELLs' home cultures. ELLs have enough to think about without wondering what they did to make their teacher talk to them that way. Advanced students have a better grasp of these nuances, but it may take a while.

ESOL students also have a hard time with negative statements and questions. In many cultures, agreement with a negative statement warrants a positive, as in "Yes, that negative statement is true." In English, we use a negative to agree with a negative, as in, "My 'no' goes with your 'no.'" Keep it simple and avoid using negative statements or questions with Beginning and Intermediate ELLs. Advanced students may understand better, but be aware that there may be lingering confusion.

Say this: *Raise your hand if you finished your work.*

Not this: *Raise your hand if you didn't finish your work.*

or

Question: *"Don't you want to go?"*

Answer (American English): *"No, I don't want to go."*

Answer (some other languages):*"Yes, that's right. I don't want to go."*

Advanced ESOL students will be able to appreciate most humor, but use it sparingly with Beginning and Intermediate students. If something is obviously funny or there's a visual to support it for ESOL students, it can sometimes be a language building block instead of a stumbling block. When students start making their own jokes (see Anastasia's door comment in chapter 1), they are well on their way to being proficient in English. The same is true for complex sentence structures. As students move up through the proficiency levels, it's okay to use conjunctions as you normally would. Before that point, though, a string of ideas with lots of connectors in one sentence will just obscure the meaning for your ELLs.

Figurative language can be another tough call, especially for students who are still getting their feet under them. Understanding American idioms is a skill for students at the higher Intermediate and Advanced proficiency levels. Idioms require definition and practice. Some common American idioms that mid-to-high ESOL students may be able to start with are:

- Pitch in
- Hang in there
- Sit tight
- So far, so good
- On the ball
- On thin ice
- Ring a bell
- Watch out
- Rule of thumb
- Heads up
- Under the weather
- Chin up
- Get over it
- Hit the books

Teachers of young students have experience reaching kids who are, for various reasons, not quite "there" yet. They have many of the pointers in this chapter in their collections of ready and effective strategies. Many lower grades are designed and function as language-rich environments, and that works for everybody. Talk to the kids and let them talk to each other.

Remembering the Lesson Learned from the Introduction not to assume that kids understand you, let the following illustrate being specific about how you expect students to respond:

Miss Rogers was working with Kindergarten students on vocabulary for parts of the face, and how the face can show how people feel. She told her students to touch their faces, assuming they would feel their noses, mouths, and so on. She asked the class, "What do you have on your faces?" As a whole they answered, "Hands."

KEY TAKEAWAYS

- Slow your speech rate and pause between parts of the message.
- Enunciate and avoid reductions.
- Look at the ESOL kids when you talk to the class.
- Repeat, restate, demonstrate.
- Give a heads-up/thinking time to ELs before asking them to talk in group.
- Extend your wait time for responses.
- Start with simple tenses, then move into progressive tenses.
- Speak in the active voice.
- Support meaning with facial expressions and body language.
- Use visuals and realia as much as possible.
- Create speaking opportunities for ELLs in class and informally.
- Keep it simple—avoid negatives, sarcasm, most humor, and idioms.

FIVE

Classroom Accommodations for ESOL Students

WHAT ARE ACCOMMODATIONS?

Accommodations are changes in presentation, timing, seating, workload, product, or other interaction between the student and learning environment. Accommodations are meant to minimize the language-based hurdles of new material and how kids demonstrate learning. They're supposed to help students understand and to provide a realistic picture of what they know. They are not changes made to the instructional material itself; those are modifications. Most ESOL students don't receive formal modifications.

Elementary schools have specialists on staff who have valuable insights and skills in helping kids adjust and move forward, and who are an important part of the team working with ESOL students. The classroom and ESOL teachers will want to be in contact with each other, the counselor, reading specialist, and speech and language specialist.

Typical Accommodations

- Adjusted workload – The student does not have to finish as much work as most of the class. Acceptable work can be whatever a student is able to do within a given time frame, or a certain number of responses, pages, sections, and so forth. This is especially helpful for students in pull-out ESOL programs, so they are not expected to do all the classroom work they might miss, in addition to the work from ESOL class. ESOL kids are working during their specialized instruction, usually on skills that support or align with the classroom work, so it's okay to allow them leeway with the classroom work. It is not a good idea to keep these kids in from recess or to assign extra homework to have them catch up.
- Differentiated product – EL students may show understanding in ways that are different from the general assignment. They use either nonlanguage or passive skills, or may do something in their own areas of strength using Gardner's Multiple Intelligences (http://multipleintelligencesoasis.org/). See Appendix A: Basic Skills Chart for Gardner's Multiple Intelligences.
- Extended time – ELs are untimed, or are given extra time to complete tasks or take tests.
- Monitoring – A teacher or other adult/older student helps the EL student keep track of where he or she is on the page. This is especially helpful for students who have basic literacy skills in a first language that does not read top-to-bottom, left-to-right as English does, and for students who are still learning to visually sort and recognize letters and words.
- Reduced distractions – ELs are given instruction in small groups instead of or in addition to whole-class instruction. This helps the teacher find and focus on what's needed. It gives ESOL students more of a chance to ask and answer questions, and keeps them engaged. Students who are left to their own devices while the teacher is busy easily become "unemployed" and distracted and/or

distracting. Small-group instruction for ELs can't always be available, but it works well when possible.

During testing, this often means having small groups in separate test sessions or rooms. During instruction, it's a matter of course that teachers use small groups for math and language arts instruction. It can also translate to having ELs work with one or two peers or a support adult/older student in the room.

- Read-to – A computer or human reader reads aloud to the ESOL student. Some computers come with text-to-talk features, and some programs are available to schools through subscriptions. Computer read-to programs often have helpful options for rereading or asking simple follow-up questions.

A word of caution here that read-to is not always the best bet if the student has no idea what the words mean. If a native Malayalam speaker were to read Malayalam text to a completely non-Malayalam listener, however slowly and carefully, it would just be a string of confusing sounds that still wouldn't make sense. The person who is being read to must have a foundation in listening to English language for the read-to accommodation to have instructional or assessment value. If the purpose of the read-to is to help build those skills, then it is most effective as one-to-one or in a very small group.

Read-to is not an appropriate accommodation for a student who has or appears to have an auditory processing problem.

- Repetition – The student may hear the instructions or questions more than once. The student may hear the instructions or questions more than once. In formal assessment, the repetition must be word-for-word as written. Informally, it's okay to "translate" the directions or questions to language and examples that the EL student will understand and be able to work with.
- Scribe – The student dictates responses to a teacher or other trained adult. In formal assessment settings, the transcriber must write *exactly* what the student says. In some situations, the student must then go back and tell the scribe where to put capital letters and punctuation, and how to spell certain words. It can be complicated. Some schools use computer talk-to-text programs that type as the student speaks. Informally, especially in small groups, an ESOL student can offer a verbal response. The scribe will help the student restate it correctly, write it correctly for the student, and then have the student trace or near-point copy it.

WHO IS PART OF THE ACCOMMODATIONS PROCESS?

Federal law requires appropriate accommodations for all ELLs. Schools work within federal guidelines and state rules for assigning, recording, and using accommodations. In most systems, this means a formal meeting of pertinent school-based staff, usually by the end of the first marking period. Teachers need that time to get to know their kids and to figure out which accommodations are appropriate for which students. For more information on schools' obligations to EL students, visit https://www2.ed.gov/about/offices/list/ocr/ellresources.html.

Accommodations are usually based on input from

- teachers,
- the English-acquisition specialist,
- other professionals as determined by school administration, and
- (sometimes) parents/guardians.

Most districts have standardized ways for documenting who was part of the accommodations decision, which accommodations each student is to receive, under which instructional/assessment circumstances, and who is responsible for providing them. In general, any staff member who works with EL students has to use the assigned accommodations.

The school test coordinator most often takes care of arranging the accommodations meetings, documenting decisions, and filing the necessary paperwork. The ESOL specialist, however, may handle it for just the ESOL students.

WHEN AND WHERE DO ESOL STUDENTS USE ACCOMMODATIONS?

ESOL kids get their accommodations whenever and wherever they're in learning situations at school. ELLs are entitled to their accommodations during any and all school learning or in particular subject classes as noted on the accommodations record.

Accommodations have a shelf life of one calendar year (so they include summer school or year-round schedules). A new academic year means a new set of meetings and decisions about ELL accommodations. Many teachers use the previous year's documentation to help them get started with their ESOL students and to figure out if changes are needed.

Accommodations during instruction and formative assessment may look different from how they look during summative assessments and "big tests," but are essentially the same. State oversight about accommodations during high-stakes testing makes school- and district-level documentation very important.

The point of accommodations, though, is not only to help kids take big tests, but to make every-day learning and demonstration of learning less confounding. Students who are eligible for an ESOL program, but whose adults opt them out (inactive), are eligible for the same accommodations as EL students in a program (active).

Students who have exited (finished/"passed") a formal ESOL program are called Reassigned English Learners (RELs). Individual states use federal guidelines to decide if RELs may receive accommodations and what those may be.

WHY USE ACCOMMODATIONS?

Accommodations are meant to help ELLs clear the hurdle of incomplete language skills. They create a freer flow of information between ELs and teachers. ESOL students often find it difficult to demonstrate what they know and can be frustrated enough to quit trying. Accommodations help keep them in the learning stream and making progress. These students are trying to learn the same content as their classmates and master a new language and culture at the same time. It's a lot. Accommodations help them:

- Understand content
- Finish assignments
- Improve their English
- Feel comfortable and included in class

KEY TAKEAWAYS

- Accommodations are guided by federal law, defined at the state and district levels, and determined at the school level.
- All ESOL students are entitled to accommodations, whether or not they are in ESOL programs.
- School specialists are valuable assets to the EL, and classroom and ESOL teachers.
- A school-based professional team will determine EL accommodations.
- Accommodations are reviewed once a year.
- All school staff who work with ELs are responsible for using the assigned accommodations.
- Accommodations for EL students are relevant throughout the school day, in all instructional settings.
- Exited ESOL students might receive accommodations, according to their state rules.
- Accommodations help provide a true picture of what EL students know and can do.

SIX

Making the Puzzle Pieces Fit

THE BASICS

Information from previous chapters will help teachers and their ESOL students have smooth and productive school days. To recap, the basics are:

- Learn what you can about your ELs, their cultures, and their individual stories.
- Learn how to pronounce their names.
- Expect behavioral stumbles.
- Know their levels in the four language-acquisition domains.
- Adjust oral language to clear, shorter utterances in slower, active voice with repetition.
- Adjust written language to shorter sentences with bigger, wider letters and spaces.
- Front-load vocabulary.
- Use artifacts and visuals as much as possible.
- Use individual EL accommodations.
- Allow different or differentiated products.

First Steps

The Teacher

Elementary-school teachers typically create warm, welcoming, unscary-as-possible environments and teach kids to be nice and to help each other. If the new student is coming after the year starts and there's time before the student arrives, talk to the kids about the new friend coming in who is still learning to speak English. Chances are that many of the students will want to talk about times when they were new to something or felt lonesome or nervous, so they will understand how the new kid might feel and want to help.

If the student joins the class at the beginning of the school year, their adjustment might be a little easier, since everyone is getting the same new information at the same time, and it will all likely be repeated and practiced. Check frequently with new EL students to see how well or poorly they're keeping up with understanding and learning the standard operating procedures.

Choose a few helpers (see "The Buddy System" in this chapter) and take a limited tour of the school places that the new ESOLer will need right away: the bathroom, lunchroom/cafeteria, playground, other grade-level classrooms, dismissal exits, etc. Name each place, and if possible, introduce the new student to the adults in each place. Let them know that the student is learning English, what language the student speaks, and the student's name. The new student doesn't have to talk or say hello unless they want to. Start with a few places and build until the new EL has seen all the school locations they will need.

Teachers should use simple language to name places and actions until they have a good idea of what the new ESOL student can manage in English. They should stay very close at hand during the new arrival's first few lunches, dismissals, and transitions to specials in order to introduce the student to the specialists and any emergency drills.

Provide, if possible, a grade-level-appropriate picture dictionary for each new ESOL student to have for use throughout the day. Kids can point to pictures for the teacher and/or buddies to name and to indicate something they need. If it's apparent that the EL has a question or something to say, let the student use the pictures or words as much as he or she can, then the teacher should say what the student wants in standard English. Give the new ESOL student a composition or spiral notebook with pencils and colored pencils or crayons to use as desired.

Dismissals can be unnerving for new ESOL students. Find out how the student is getting home and help the student find siblings or other family members at the end of the day. A younger kid will need help getting to walking/driving pick-up zones. New ELs might also be worried about getting on the wrong bus or missing their stop. If possible, find an older student who rides the same bus to help make sure the new kid gets on the right one and meets the driver. Staff may be able to get bus information from the school office, introduce the new ESOL student to the driver, and double-check the drop-off point.

During instruction, front-load the vocabulary in as many modes as possible—say it, write it, demonstrate it, portray it with items or pictures, and have kids write and/or repeat it. As you write each word, say the letters and then read the word. Use different colors for different words, if you can. Post the corresponding picture next to the new word or put a label on the item in the room. Keep the list and items available for the duration of the topic. As kids progress, or if it works for the group, students may do the naming, writing/labeling, and reading.

Writing or copying along with the teacher can be one of the uses of the composition book or spiral notebook given to the new student when they came in. Make sure students know to date each page they use. The dates help the teacher use the student entries as an informal assessment tool and to show progress or lack thereof over time. Photocopy pages to save as work samples (a mandate in some districts). Students keep their composition books at the end of the year to remind them of how far they've come.

Figure 6.1.   Sample kindergarten composition book page, midyear, no date. The page is folded to make two columns, one for each target word. The teacher gave verbal directions while modeling the page on chart paper. The heading is far-point copied, but the target words were traced so the student had time to finish the drawings. Letter shape and spacing is good; position and relative size need work. Created by author.

Use the say-write-demonstrate-read strategy when asking questions: Say the question first, then write and read each individual word, then reread the whole question sentence. As noted in the previous chapter, give ESOLers a heads-up about any questions that will be directed at them. Accept the answer at whatever level of English the ESOL student has, and restate it correctly for Beginners and Intermediate students. In a small group, ask the ESOL student/s to try to repeat it correctly; it's usually more effective if they can repeat the sentence in fragments rather than all at once. It may be slow going at first.

Back to that hard-working hen.

Teacher*: What is the hen doing?*

Student*: He broomin' she house.*

Teacher: *That's right! She is sweeping her house/porch/kitchen/floor. This is a broom.* (Point to the picture.)

Everybody point to the picture of the broom. Say "broom."

(Write and spell "broom" on the board.)

*You use a **broom** to **sweep.***

(Write "sweep" on the board.)

Everybody say "sweep."

(If your kids know nouns and verbs, you can reinforce them here.)

Where can you see a real broom? (kitchen, cafeteria, store)

Stand up with me and pretend to use a broom to sweep. Good. Sit down and say it after me. "She is . . . "

Student/s: *She is . . .*

Teacher: *. . . sweeping her house . . .*

Student/s: *. . . sweepin' her house . . .*

Teacher: *. . . with a broom.*

Student/s: *. . . wif a broom.*

Teacher: *Let's do the whole thing. Remember to say all the letter sounds in i-n-g so it's sweep**ing**, not sweep**in'**, and **with**, not wif.*

(Write "sweep**ing**" and "wi**th**" on the board).

Say after me, "She is sweeping her house with a broom."

Student/s: *She is sweeping her house with a broom.*

Teacher: *Does anyone want to try it alone and say the "ing" and "th" sounds?* or *Let's practice the "ing" and "th" together. Sweep**ing** . . . wi**th**. Remember to THtick your tongue out a little bit for "th"!*

. . . and so on. If kids still have trouble with certain sounds, let it go after two or three tries. Say, *"That's better! We'll work on it again next time"*, or *"Very close! We'll do some more next time."*

The Buddy System

Teachers often have buddies ready for any new kids joining the class. For ELs, it makes the transition to all this new stuff far easier, especially if it's possible to pair them with someone who has similar interests or background. If two kids are wearing basketball shirts or have the same animated character lunchbox, that's a good match as they are already likely to have something in common. Chances are that there will be lots of volunteers and some who tend to hover and overhelp, so it's good to let kids take turns.

Buddies should have specific jobs and/or time-frame assignments, mostly designed to help the new ESOL student feel less lost and to start naming everyday objects. They give new students someone to sit with in class and at lunch to connect with on the playground, to help them find things in the classroom, and to keep them from getting lost in the building. Allow buddies to help with classwork, too, and to talk to the new ESOL student as they would talk to any other classmate. ESOL students can help their buddies with classroom jobs.

Be aware when assigning buddies that there can be animosity between different areas of the same home country, or between different cultures that seem to share a language. Some widespread languages from around the world have been localized enough that other speakers don't understand them. Spanish from Spain, the Philippines, South America, Central America, and North America is a good example. Portuguese from Portugal is different from Portuguese from Brazil, as are the many dialects among Mandarin Chinese speakers. This is a good place to apply the early "never assume" lesson.

There are more sources for teachers looking for other specific strategies, including *Pathways to Teaching Series: Practical Strategies for Teaching English Language Learners* by Ellen M. Curtin and *Phonics that Work! New Strategies for the Reading/Writing Classroom* by Janiel M. Wagstaff.

TECHNOLOGY FOR THE UNEMPLOYED

As noted in an earlier chapter, ESOL students who can't manage classwork can easily disengage and, purposely or not, be distracted or distracting. It's impossible and unrealistic in a typical elementary classroom for staff to be 100 percent available 100 percent of the time, even to the most needy language learners. If a classroom has computers, there are many online sites that can help your language learners get and stay productive. The building media specialist, reading specialist, ESOL specialist, and/or teammates may have great suggestions for sites to use with ELs in the classroom. Check them out before giving kids access. A few are listed here to help teachers and their ESOL students get started.

- https://www.education.com/games, Beginner–Intermediate (requires membership)
  Interactive alphabet and vocabulary learning games and videos that can be sorted by grade, and Math or Reading/Language Arts. It has a section about idioms, and over thirty vocabulary topics. The site includes other learning and printable plans and materials.
- https://www.gamestolearnenglish.com/spelling-bee-english/ with audio, Beginner–Intermediate
  Online and interactive smart board vocabulary and spelling games and a **picture dictionary with audio and print** arranged by topic (bottom of the page, under the game icons). There is also a short picture dictionary in Spanish, and a set of Chinese characters.
- https://www.eslgamesplus.com/classroom-games/, High Beginner — Intermediate
  Thirty-five interactive vocabulary and grammar games with sound effects. The following is a breakdown of what's available on this site for Intermediate kids.

Vocabulary

actions	colors	numbers	shapes and sizes
animals	countries	numbers 1–10	space/solar system
bathroom	food	quantity	sports
bedroom	fruit	school subjects	vegetables
clothes	jobs/tools	school supplies	weather

Grammar

adjectives	present tense - progressive
affixes (prefixes/suffixes)	present tense - simple
past tense - irregular	verbs
prepositions	verb tenses

LET'S DO LUNCH — BOOK TALK

This activity is a favorite with ELs and native English speakers alike, and often with the teachers who use it. As background, it was initiated by this writer many years ago as a way to maximize time with ESOL students in the three elementary schools that shared one ESOL teacher allocation. Travel time and a tangle of other peoples' schedules took a big bite out of English language instruction, but a little creative time management went a long way.

Classroom teachers are no strangers to surprises or interruptions, and trying to fit sixty minutes of work into twenty minutes, so the Book Talk program offers some possibilities for staying close to reading/ language arts instructional time guidelines. Initially, it was necessary to get the okay of building administrators for the Book Talk time to count toward the state recommended number of minutes of language instruction per week, and to give the teacher some flexibility. Once it got going, though, and the benefits were obvious, it became a regular part of the schools' ESOL programs. Numerous studies support the value of read-alouds, particularly to ELLs.

Book Talk started as a one-teacher-three-schools program, but as more ESOL and classroom teachers in multiple schools, and then in multiple systems, saw its success, they adapted it to their needs. It is generally used as part of an ESOL program, but input from classroom teachers is an important piece and classroom teachers can use it, too.

Overview

Book Talk is described here as part of an ESOL teacher's day, but is adaptable for classroom teachers. If a grade-level team is trying this, teachers can take turns on a weekly basis.

Book Talk is a lunch bunch for English Language Learners. The setup and "rules" can be flexible depending on time, space, and number of students. It's understood that a classroom teacher is probably giving up a lunch or planning time to do this, but an ESOL specialist can make it part of the ESOL schedule and fit it around their lunch and planning, as well as the many times that students are not available for English class.

For an ESOL teacher with multiple grades, Book Talk for every English Learner in grades 1–5 means two different lunch groups a day for several days. For a classroom teacher or team, it means one teacher lunchtime per week, or however many weeks equal the number of teammates who want to try it.

Once a week, the teacher has lunch with the ESOL students in each grade or in whatever configuration the groups meet. Depending on available space, the groups can include REL students and/or having ELs each invite a non-ESOL friend from their class. If space is crowded, one or two ESOLers a week, on a rotating basis, may bring one friend each. For several years in one particular school, students who had exited ESOL by third grade continued to ask for Book Talk through fifth grade, even though there were no longer any active ESOL kids in their class.

Kids take their lunches to the ESOL or other available classroom and eat while the teacher reads aloud. The ESOL teacher can choose books or stories for fun, or that support the skills the group needs, or can check with the classroom teachers for genres, stories, topics, or authors they're covering in class.

Kindergarten students don't participate, since they aren't mature enough to manage the transitions. All proficiency levels in grades 1–3 and all Beginning–Intermediate students in grades 4–5 are expected to be part of Book Talk. If grades 4 and 5 share a lunch/recess time and there is a manageable number of them, they can attend Book Talk together. Advanced students in grades 4 and 5 may opt out. Mondays aren't generally a good day for Book Talk because so many holidays are on Mondays, and kids lose that time.

Before—Setting Up

Tell the classroom teachers that their ELs will be eating lunch in the ESOL room with the ESOL teacher. Let them know which day, and make sure it works for them. If there's no ESOL room, or the room is too small, work with staff to find a room that's available for you to use at the time needed, preferably close to the lunchroom. Promise to clean up!

Tell the cafeteria and lunchroom staff that you will be picking up your ESOLers during their lunchtime on X day. If possible, get the kids who are coming to Book Talk close to the front of the buyers' line. Some lunchroom assistants will help them hurry up and remember to meet the Book Talk teacher, or will find the kids who have already sat down at tables.

Check with lunchroom staff to find a place where you can meet the Book Talk kids, and where they will know to go with their lunches. They may not, as a rule, go to the Book Talk room on their own.

Get a large, lined trashcan to use on Book Talk days. Lunches can get messy, so to avoid making extra work for building service staff, the kids must be 100 percent responsible for cleaning up after themselves. If the school recycles lunch trays, have kids stack them on the table, and assign a pair of kids per group to take them back to the lunchroom.

Keep a supply of straws, napkins, condiment packets, and plastic utensils in the room. (Kids forget this stuff and it saves trips back to the lunchroom.) Have disinfectant wipes in large containers.

During—Let's Eat

Once in the room, kids just sit and eat while the teacher reads. It's easier for them to see the pictures and read the teacher's facial expressions if everyone is at a small-group table, but, as always, this depends on available space. Kids may need to be at desks, and in a few cases, this writer's groups ate "picnic style" on big sheets of construction paper on the floor. It's not uncommon for kids to become entranced and forget their food, so the teacher has to remind them to keep eating. For ELs who are bringing food from home that looks and smells different from most public school lunches, Book Talk makes that OK. They can see how many other kids also have different kinds of foods.

Kids are allowed to toss out questions or make connections or comments—anything that feels authentic to them as listeners. Teachers will know which interruptions to accept and which to ask kids to hold on to for a minute. There have been occasional times when a guest behaves badly; in that case, the teacher "uninvites" them for future Book Talks.

There's a lot of language going on during Book Talk, and not just between the reader and the listeners. Kids relax to talk to each other, and talk informally and extemporaneously to the teacher. Casual talk with the teacher and conversations between kids begets a lot of information about what's going on in kids' lives and what's on their minds. There's a nice space here, too, to have students demonstrate their home languages. During one second-grade Book Talk, two African boys happened to sit next to each other. They were not in the same class, and one of them was new to the school.

Teacher: *Look at the cat on top of the refrigerator! Yoseph, how do you say "cat" in Amharic?*

Yoseph answered, and the new boy said something back to Yoseph in Amharic.

Yoseph (jumping out of his chair): *Hey! He a Eth'opia boy ju' like me!"*

Book Talk is also a good time to teach or reinforce basic manners. An earlier chapter mentioned a large extended family of siblings and cousins managed by eight-year-old Marco. To a person, that group had no idea how to behave at a table—lots of grabbing, eating with fingers, yelling over each other, and so on. It was an easy addition to their language learning and social skills during Book Talk to add, "May I please have . . .", "Please pass the . . .", "Thank you," and "You're welcome," and to learn how to hold and use utensils (not like holding a toothbrush) and napkins. There are times, too, when Young Princes and Princesses have to learn how to clean up after themselves.

After — Clean Up

Clean up starts three to five minutes before the end of the lunch period. All liquids go into the nearest sink and are rinsed down the drain. All trash goes into the big trash can. Every student cleans up his or her own space, including the table, chair, and floor. A volunteer will usually offer to wipe down the table with a disinfectant wipe. Have kids check for their lunchboxes, coats, and so on. If kids go to recess after lunch, they may leave their lunchboxes in the room and collect them afterward. If the ESOL room is closed, the teacher can leave kids' things outside the door.

Kids are *very* disappointed if Book Talk has to be cancelled. If the teacher knows ahead of time, the kids should have a heads-up and the teacher should try to reschedule. Other teachers also offer Lunch Bunch times, and it's OK for ELs to miss Book Talk for those special times with their teachers.

The Book Talk Ripple Effect

The titles from the suggested readings in Appendix B are popular with kids and teachers alike, and because many are from prolific writers, it's easy for kids to get them for independent reading (or "reading") from the school or public library. One second-grade boy who struggled across the board was all about Book Talk. About halfway through the school year, he started asking the school media specialist for copies of books he had heard in Book Talk so he could read them to his baby brother. Another student would get Magic Tree House books from the Media Center to read ahead, with the promise that he wouldn't tell the endings.

A group of third graders organized a Kate DiCamillo quiz game at the end of the year, with game rules and questions that they wrote themselves. In a middle school with very few readers, the kids worked together to make cartoon panels from the *Hatchet* books the teacher had read to them. Schools want to generate independent readers and joy in reading. Book Talk contributes to those goals.

If you are part of a team, or your ESOL teacher is doing the Book Talk program, work together to find titles that relate to upcoming topics. This goes back to front-loading vocabulary, but with the addition of concepts and context. More than once, a classroom teacher would visit the ESOL room and say something like, "We were talking about habitats today, and Omar said, 'We heared about this in Book Talk!' Thank you!" or "We read a story by X author, and Juliana told me she knew about him from Book Talk."

Kids often request books or stories, but the teacher has to look them over before agreeing to add them to the reading list. Sometimes a student will want to be a Guest Reader, which, again, is up to the teacher. Guest Readers from among the staff are a big hit, especially if the staff members are not teachers. It demonstrates that lots of people like reading, and that it's fun.

See Appendix B for suggested Book Talk titles by grade level.

KEY TAKEAWAYS

- Stay close to the new ESOL student for the first couple of days, especially during transitions or safety drills.
- Take the student on a brief school tour and introduce staff that you encounter.
- Make picture dictionaries available (try Oxford University Press or Longman versions).
- Give each one a composition book or spiral notebook to write in, along with pencils and coloring tools.
- Assign a rotating group of buddies for the regular Standard Operating Procedure stuff and as work partners.
- Get programs for learning English loaded onto the classroom computer/s.
- Use the strategies from chapter 4, "How to Talk to Your ELLs."
- Use the allowed EL accommodations from chapter 5, "Classroom Accommodations for ESOL Students," especially wait time, reduced workload, and differentiated products.

- Eat lunch and read aloud once a week to ELs, in a version of Book Talk that works for your classroom.

SEVEN
Project-Based Learning

WHY PBL?

Project-Based Learning (PBL) has many definitions, all of them centered on the idea that kids can work in teams, on long-term projects, to understand authentic content and show what they know. At its heart, PBL is a way to get students into engaging and active learning. It has extra importance for ELLs because it provides common experiences among themselves and with their classmates, helps fill in background information, builds language structure, and adds to vocabulary. PBL is a way for ESOL students to stay afloat in the same learning stream as their classmates and practice new language without a spotlight.

For ELL purposes, Project-Based Learning can also be considered *Product*-Based Learning. Earlier chapters talked about the value of hands-on, real-world experiences for ELs, and most of the projects that follow are designed around items that kids can show and talk/write about. They also have the often-unrecognized value of fun.

PBL activities can get up and running at the school's and/or teacher's discretion. The most practical way to build them is from pieces that kids already have to study or master. PBL work can be large or small group, modified, or adjusted as needed, and on a timeline that's practical for the group/s. In addition to vocabulary, each activity offers a wealth of language learning, but it's better to focus on only one new skill per project. Sample PBL language objectives for ESOL students are listed below:

Special Groups

A first-grade ESOL student asked one day what "Spessuhlimbix" were, after he heard some special education teachers say it. The ESOL class talked about the special-education programs in the school to make the connection to Special Olympics. Students in grades 1–3 joined a project from the Smithsonian Institution's National Postal Museum to have school kids write letters of encouragement to Special Olympic athletes. They worked from vocabulary and sentence starters posted in the ESOL room. (This is context for the "I would get clobbered" remark in chapter 3.)

Make Something

Prime considerations for making something are cost, how much prep it needs, how messy it will be, and how long it will take. Keep in mind the availability of a working sink.

Much of the time, classes make things around the December holidays as gifts for people important to them. Some things are season or other holiday based, especially if the holiday is new to the ELs, like Halloween and Thanksgiving. Document the process with pictures, as they help students with the end-of-project writing activities and make them bulletin-board worthy.

- Making a list
- Procedures

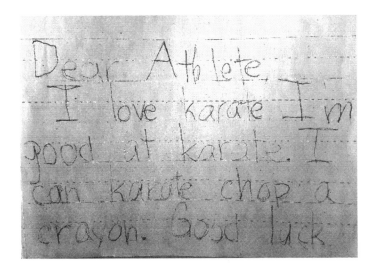

Figure 7.1.   Student letter to a Special Olympian. Created by author.

- Transition words
- Key words and note taking
- Before - During - After
- Opinions
- Nouns and verbs
- Pronouns
- Subject - Verb - Object agreement
- Prepositions
- Regular and irregular past tense
- Regular and irregular plurals

The following examples are loosely arranged by what kids can **do**. They are meant to help teachers find projects and products for their own classrooms. Most of them work easily in small groups, or with the whole class divided into small groups that each have specific tasks or whose group members have specific tasks. And, of course, every activity will have its share of not-surprising surprises while kids are working on them.

Collect Something

The class can collect something that another group needs or something just for fun. In these examples, the groups that started each project were able to involve other classes and parts of their communities. They gave kids perspective beyond their limited circles at home, church, or school. The projects helped them start thinking outside themselves and to see that they were part of something beyond the familiar walls they looked at every day.

Postcards

A set of donated postcards found its way into the picture file in the ESOL room. The third-grade group looked through them and decided to do a Postcard Project. Using the world map as inspiration, the teacher and class planned to collect one hundred postcards from as many places as possible by the end of the school year. (This can be adapted for one hemisphere, one continent, one country, and/or a different time frame.)

- The group composed a blurb for the staff bulletin and the PTA newsletter. They asked people to tell other folks about the project and gave out the school address, with attention to ESOL.

- They posted a giant sheet of one-hundred-square paper and numbered the boxes, left to right, top to bottom. Students took turns writing in the numbers at intervals of ten.
- They posted a seven-column chart with the continents as headings.
- Miss Rogers got push pins and string for putting the postcards on the map (along the outside perimeter).
- Once a week, kids tacked postcards to the map, colored in the appropriate number of spaces on the one-hundred-square paper, and wrote the name of each place and the sender under the correct continent on the chart.
- At intervals, students wrote in their composition books about which cards came in, how the sender found out about the project, their favorite postcards, and so on.

This project took longer than one year, so the kids who started it—including the kids who would be exiting ESOL—asked to continue it into the next school year. In a classroom, the project can transfer to the incoming class. It has any number of cross-curricular connections, especially in social studies and language arts, a little bit of math, and possibilities for art and music.

There were several well-traveled people who contributed a lot of postcards to the project. When the class recognized this, each kid started keeping tallies on a dedicated page in their composition book that listed the Major Contributors names, one tally mark per postcard. If they got more than three to five postcards from the same person, the group sent a thank-you message directly through e-mail, or through the person who led them to the project. One of the most generous contributors was a staff member in the building, so she got a special letter at the end of the school year. All the kids who participated across the two academic years of collecting postcards were allowed to take them home at the end of the project. The kids drew numbers to see what order they'd go in, round-robin, to choose cards from the map.

Write to Someone

Some letter-writing projects are continuous through the school year, but if schedules require something more short-term, they can be as simple as the exchange of a couple of emails. The possibilities are endless, especially in social studies and science.

Figure 7.2. The Postcard Project. Created by author.

Experts

Whatever your kids are studying, find an expert about the subject in the context your group needs and get in touch. Almost everyone's professional contact information is available online. Remember to use only the professional information available through the person's website, employment address, or agent.

- Use the expert's material and other research to take notes in composition books. (Keywords, phrases, and sketches suffice.)
- Help kids brainstorm a list of important words or ideas and write questions in their composition books, then use them to make a group K-W-L (**K**now - **W**ant to know - **L**earned) chart.
- With the group, compile the questions into a polite note to the expert, asking for answers.
- Use the information from the expert to build a class activity with differentiated products.

Miss Rogers has a family member who works for NASA in their crewed (manned) spaceflight program, and who was a content editor for a book about the International Space Station. The second-grade ESOL class used the book and student parts of the NASA website to do research and generate questions to send him. They were thrilled to get specific answers.

The kids drew pictures from their research about space exploration. They wrote captions and posted them in the hallway, with a copy of the questions and answers. This project was easy to repeat for several years as different second-graders came in, since the expert continued to work in Mission Control and to be Miss Rogers's son.

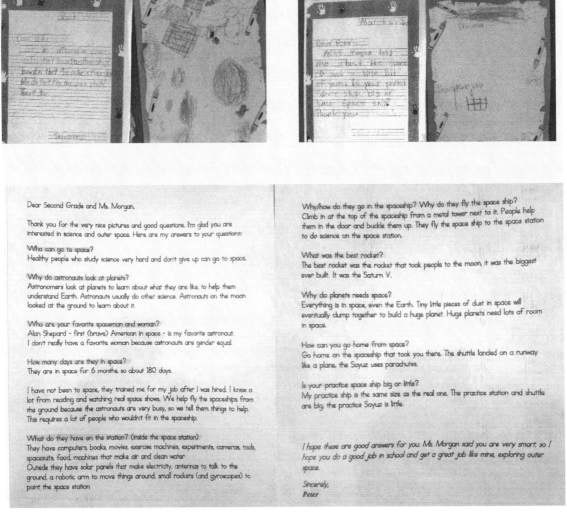

Figure 7.3.   Letters between students and an outer space expert. Created by author.

Snack Mix (One to Two Sessions)

Be aware of dietary restrictions and allergies! Kids can tell you what they like and usually what they can't eat. Vegetarian students cannot have anything with gelatin, like gummy candies. Be aware that many cultures find American snacks too sweet and don't like them, so check with your students' parents or guardians before you decide on ingredients. Some suggestions:

- Small pretzels
- Raisins and/or other dried fruit
- Goldfish crackers
- Chocolate candies (chips or M&M's®)
- Peanuts (*only* if no one in the room has a peanut allergy!)

Provide unbreakable bowls, large spoons, resealable sandwich bags, goody bags, tape, gift tag stickers, and paper towels/napkins. Pour each snack into a separate bowl with two large spoons. Give each student a paper towel. On each paper towel, put one of each snack for students to taste.

Kids take turns, one rotation per snack bowl, putting one spoonful of whatever they choose into their snack bags. If there's enough, kids can use more scoops of some ingredients or make another bag for themselves. Make sure the bags are sealed.

For gift snacks, put filled sealed bags into larger goody bags, one per one. Gather the top of the goody bag, wrap a ribbon around it, and tie it in a double bow to keep it closed. Have each student tell you who the snack is for so you can make a To/From gift sticker for each student's bag.

Put the snacks directly into backpacks to go home. Follow-up with a procedural writing activity.

A Booklet After Interviews with Staff Members (Requires a Camera and Three to Five Sessions)

ESOL book projects use limited technology as a way to provide multimodal practice. Teachers may use technology at their own discretion, but for building language, handwritten projects create stronger memory pathways for vocabulary, usage, and mechanics.

This project is an interview between early grade students (usually Kindergartners) and volunteer staff members. You may have to arrange with Kindergarten teachers to pull a few students out of class at irregular times to do their interviews when the staff members are free. The interview is designed to help ESOL students follow multistep directions, ask and answer "wh" questions, listen, and practice speaking and writing. Make a question and answer template that can be used year after year.

Questions (Choose one of each "wh" question, or write others, with input from kids).

1. Who are the people in your family? Who do you work with at our school?
2. What is your job at school? What do you like best about your job?

Figure 7.4.   Kindergarten students interview staff volunteers. Created by author.

3. When did you start to work in a school? When did you start to work at our school?
4. Where are you from? Where do you like to go for vacation? Where do you live?
5. Why did you pick the job you have? Why do you work at our school?
6. What else do you want me to know about you? What else do you want to tell me?

Practice reading the questions as a group and with individual students. Assign the interview pairs and schedule their time, based on staff availability. Have students copy or fill in a request/invitation that includes the date, time, and place.

Dear _____,
    I am a Kindergarten ESOL student. We are learning about people at our school. Will you please let me interview you? Please come to __ (room)___on __(date)__ at __(time)__.
Thank you,
    _____ (student name)

Have each student copy his or her staff person's name on the front of an envelope and take the kids with you to deliver the notes to staff mailboxes. Sometimes kids get written replies! Several pairs can work at the same time in different parts of the room, for twenty to thirty minutes.

The interview pair sits together to complete the questionnaire. Subjects may help with the reading and generate conversation by asking the students the same questions. Take a picture of each interview pair. You will need two copies of each picture. The subject helps the student write key words to the subject's answers.

After the interview, they read the key words and compose sentences together. The teacher transcribes the student's sentences onto the original questionnaire. Each student then copies the sentences onto a clean questionnaire. Make one extra copy—two copies if the teacher wants to save one as a Listening and/ or Speaking work sample. Each student chooses a color for the cover (each cover is half of a full sheet of construction paper, folded in half along the longer side). Print a cover sheet for each.

Staff member name
A Very Special Person at _____ Elementary
by
Student name
A picture of the interviewer and staff member

Students glue their subject-self picture to the cover sheet, then glue the cover sheet to the cover and the information pages to the inside of the cover (two sets of these should be made). Make the original for the student and the copy for the interview subject. When all the booklets are ready, take the group on a walk around the school to deliver the staff copies and have each student say, "Thank you for helping me. I made this for you."

Follow with a general discussion about the project, and ask students to take their booklets home.

A Decision

Under the practical adage of "Use what you have," you may often call on friends and family to support your PBL activities. Miss Rogers's young adult children can verify the frequency with which that happens. Her daughter, Ellen, spent many December afternoons, for several years, coaching every level and grade of ESOL student in squishing polymer clay into small snowmen, bears, and penguins.

First-grade ELs had read Cynthia Rylant's wonderful story *Mr. Putter and Tabby Pour the Tea*, in which an old man adopts an old cat. Ellen agreed to ask first-grade ESOL students for help in making a decision about whether or not she should get a cat. She then asked for their input about whether or not the cat should be allowed to go outside. Miss Rogers got an email for her class:

Dear first-grade ESOL students,
    I was glad to meet you when we made your snowmen. You did a great job. I hope you can do another job with me. I want to get a cat, but I need help to decide. I know you are good thinkers. Can you please send me some good and bad ideas about having a cat? Thank you.
Sincerely,
Miss Ellen

Miss Better

A Very Special Person at
_____ Elementary
by Kindergarten ESOL Student

G A B Y

Kindergarten Interview

Student GABy
Adult Miss Better

1. Who is in your family?

Miss Better has a mom
and dad, 2 sisters and
two dogs.

2. Where is your family from?

Her family is from
Hungary.

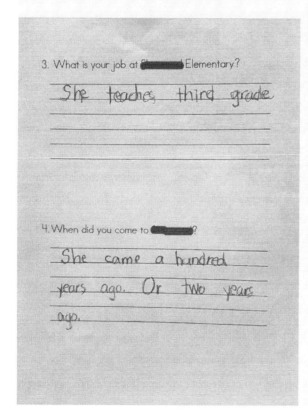

3. What is your job at _____ Elementary?

She teaches third grade

4. When did you come to _____?

She came a hundred
years ago. Or two years
ago.

5. Why do you like _____?

She loves all of the
kids and the staff that
works here.

6. What other things can you tell me about yourself?

Miss Better likes to play
sports. She went to the
University of Maryland.

Figure 7.5. Front cover and inside pages of an interview booklet. Created by author.

The class made a two-column chart (on chart paper), with one column titled "yes" and the other "no." Kids talked about the pros and cons of getting a cat. Miss Rogers wrote their ideas on the chart and then each student signed their name under the column that showed what they thought Ellen should do.

Miss Rogers sent an email to Ellen with a picture of the class's chart.

Dear Miss Ellen,

We made a list of good ideas and bad ideas for you. We think it is a good idea for you to get a cat. You would be happy. The cat would be happy, too.

Sincerely,

First-grade ESOL (names followed)

Figure 7.6.   First-grade ESOLers helped Ellen get a cat. Created by author.

Ellen answered:

Dear first-grade ESOL students,
 Thank you for helping me decide to get a cat. Her name is Sadie. She was a stray cat that my friend found under her deck. Now Sadie is an inside cat, but she still wants to go outside, too. Do you think I should let her go out?
Sincerely,
Miss Ellen

The class made another chart of reasons for letting the cat go outside and sent it in another email. Ellen emailed the class that she had decided to let Sadie go outside because she always stayed right next to the house and came when Ellen called her (and shook the treats bag).

Ellen sent the class a picture of Sadie that students posted in the hall with their charts. They posted short descriptions of how they helped Ellen make decisions about her cat.

Play Something

Dress Up, the Winter Version (Two to Four Sessions)

Young students and early ELs use general terms for most clothes. Everything with sleeves is a "yack-et," anything on the foot is a "tchoo." When the weather gets cold, kids from hot climates often don't know what to call the items they need to stay warm, so this activity can help them learn the vocabulary of different kinds of clothes.

This activity is good for:

- Adjectives
- Labels
- Categories/Compare and Contrast
- Weather/Seasons/Climate

The teacher brings in a collection of winter clothes in sizes that are too big for the students. It's best to bring multiples of each item—two or three scarves, several pairs of gloves and mittens—so kids don't have to wait to try on certain things. Post a list of clothes that are available. Suggested items:

coats with and without hoods	jackets with and without hoods	scarf/scarves
boots	hats	gloves**
mittens*	ski goggles	headbands
earmuffs (aka "ear muffins")	items with zippers***, buttons, snaps, velcro	

* Medial double "t" can be hard to pronounce. Practice to get away from "mid-den" or "mi'in" mispronunciations to the correct "mit'n." (The tip of the tongue stops on the roof of the mouth behind the front teeth, like stopping just before the final "t" sound of "didn't".) Likewise for "button," not "bud-din" or "buh'in."
** Not "glubs." Practice the "v" sound of top teeth touching the bottom lip.
*** "Zipper" is a noun, "zip" is a verb. Kids often use "zip" for both.

The teacher demonstrates and "models" each item. Allow time for students to talk about each item after the demonstration. Use leading questions to help them. Show the difference between mittens and gloves; hold hands, palms out, in front of you, then spread your fingers wide open and say "glove hands." Put your four tall fingers together with the thumbs sticking out and say "mitten hands." Give kids time to practice.

Have kids stand and bend their knees, then reach their arms down to their bent knees. Tell them that a coat ends close to their knees. Have them bend forward and put their hands where their bodies bend, at the tops of their legs. Tell them that a jacket is short and ends close to the tops of their legs. Practice the initial "j" sound. Put a hat on, take it off, and let go of it. It falls. Do the same with a hood. It doesn't fall. Have kids describe what happened.

Let kids explore (play with) the clothes, then have each one choose at least three items that they want to wear for a picture. They may have to share and wait for certain items. Take and print each student's picture. Have students glue their pictures to the top of half a sheet of picture-story paper. Talk about the pictures. Help kids post an adjective word bank: cute, funny, warm, cozy, silly, soft, fuzzy, itchy, heavy, big, loose, and so forth.

Have the students copy the clothes sentences onto their picture-story paper lines and fill in the blanks to match their pictures. Help as needed.

I am wearing _____(name the clothes)_____.
The (one item) is _____(size, color, texture)_____.
I look _____(adjective/s)_____.

Have each student use the clothes word bank to write what they wore in the clear spaces around their picture, then use a ruler to draw a line from each word to the item in their photo. Students will read their sentences to the class and tell why they chose to wear one of the items. Display the finished papers. Higher-level ESOLers may be able to take on more specific vocabulary like collar, cuff, sleeve, pocket, drawstring, shoelace, buttonhole, and so on. Kids like having a group photo in the winter gear to keep in the classroom.

Figure 7.7.   Kindergarten students playing Dress-up, the Winter Version. Created by author.

Jeopardy

A Jeopardy-like quiz game is excellent and fun practice for listening to and constructing questions, as well as noting details. It starts as ongoing note-taking about shared books or a book series. Author-study picture or short-chapter books and *The Magic Tree House* stories are easy to use for this. The teacher may want to provide a template or capture sheet. Students will know about the quiz game and can keep a countdown on the board.

As the group reads through the book/s, the teacher can take notes on the board while students do the same in their composition books or capture sheets. Notes can be based on the "wh" questions and students may help each other. Completed capture sheets are then dated, folded, and taped into composition books. A few days before the quiz game, do some practice question/answer sessions for the younger classes, or answer/questions sessions for students in grades 3 and up. The teacher will use questions based on notes and allow students to look at their notes during practice.

Kids can work in teams of two to four at the teacher's discretion. Have each group write a set number of questions with brief answers for assigned chapters or books that they may use for reference. This writing goes into the composition books. Screen and edit the questions, then have the groups write their teacher-approved questions with answers on index cards, one set per card. The teacher collects and shuffles the cards to use during the actual quiz game.

To play the game, teams sit together and go round-robin for several rotations. There can also be a "buzzer round" of ring-in rotations (provide call bells). Kids like to have a special-guest quiz master (a friendly administrator, specialist, or para-educator) read the questions. The teacher can keep score. Have certificates available for the winners. This format can also be used for holiday or biography facts. Students can write a group thank-you note to the guest quiz master and write personal response opinion pieces.

Not every PBL activity will go as well as hoped or planned but can still provide a memorable moment.

Miss Rogers used Tomie dePaola's picture book Pancakes for Breakfast *with her first- and second-grade ESOL students to talk about illustrations and character feelings. The students chose pictures and wrote captions for them, in preparation for making pancakes with Miss Rogers. When Pancake Day arrived, everything that could go wrong did, so there were no pancakes that day. Miss Rogers told her students that she felt frustrated and disappointed like the lady in the story, to which one student replied, "Yeah, and you old like her, too."*

See Appendix C, "Project-Based Learning (PBL) Activities"

KEY TAKEAWAYS

- PBL has value for all students, but especially for ELs.
- PBL provides common experiences to students of different cultures and languages.
- Project-Based Learning can also be considered Product-Based Learning.
- PBL gives ELs nonstressful language practice in all domains.
- Limit new language skills to only one or two per activity.
- Write letters to experts, travelers, authors, and friends.
- Collect something for a school, a charity, or for fun.
- Make something for someone else as a gift.
- Play games in small groups or as a class.

EIGHT
Strategies for Teaching Writing

Chapter 4 talked about why writing is often the hardest and the last of the four language domains that ELs have to master. Native English speakers may also have trouble with writing, but they have the advantage of automaticity that nonnative speakers don't. For ELs, writing can be like putting together a jigsaw puzzle with missing and slippery pieces:

- The meanings of the question words
- Content vocabulary
- Correct spelling of all the words, including past tense and plurals
- How to draw all the letters
- Where the capital letters and punctuation belong
- Word order
- What the question wants them to do
- How long the answer has to be

By the time ELs gather all the parts, at speeds that vary per student, it's very possible that they've lost track of what they're supposed to do.

Kids can often give responses verbally, but have a hard time moving the words from their mouths to their hands. The culprit is often organization. The processes in this chapter may help your students get their ideas in order more easily and improve their written products.

SUMMARIES

It's hard for kids to understand and remember when they need just key words and when they need a lot of supporting information. Summaries often get out of control and end up as retelling, with far more detail than needed. A summary-writing format based on simple steps will keep students from tangling themselves in strings of run-on sentences filled with knots of unnecessary information.

Fiction

An easy and commonly used format for writing fiction summaries is Somebody-Wants-But-So (some teachers use "Wanted" instead of "Wants," sometimes followed by "Then").

- Somebody—a main character
- Wants—the goal, what the character has to do or wants to do
- But—the problem that is in the way, keeping the Somebody from the Wants
- So—the solution to the problem and end of the story

ELs and early writers will need story-structure groundwork, as well as the content vocabulary. When kids are ready to start the writing process, the steps here will give them visual support as well as boundaries.

Model each step of the process with the same story for the whole group before setting kids loose on their own choices (from Book Talk, Silent Reading, or a familiar story). Spelling errors are OK until the last copy. Each summary takes two to four sessions.

Start with two empty, face-to-face pages in composition books, or a full piece of landscape lined paper for each student. Fold the paper/s into four columns. Head each column, one each for (1) Somebody, (2) Wants, (3) But, and (4) So. Students draw small illustrations, one for each heading, directly under the headings. Do all pictures at once. (After this step, you may do either entire columns or rows.)

Write one or two naming nouns and verbs under each picture (no sentences). Kids whisper-read their words to themselves or to partners. Under each set of words, add one or two other words that describe or embellish the previous words. Spelling errors are OK. Whisper-read as above.

Kids verbally practice putting the words into one sentence for each column. Kids may replace some of their words, as long as the new ones are relevant. They don't have to use every word. When kids feel ready, listen to their sentences and give them the thumbs-up or more support as needed.

After a thumbs-up, the student may write the sentence at the bottom of the column. When a student finishes all the sentences, read them across the page as a summary.

The following sample is *Mr. Putter and Tabby Pour the Tea*, using vocabulary from the story.

Table 8.1.   Fiction Summary Chart Sample

Somebody	Wants	But	So
picture	picture	picture	picture
Mr. Putter, man	sing, stories, tea, cat	kittens, pet store	cat, shelter, love
old, lonesome, deaf	loud, interesting	young, frisky	old, deaf, happy
Mr. Putter is an old man and he is lonesome.	He wants a cat to tell his interesting stories to and share his tea with.	But the pet store kittens are too young and frisky.	So he gets an old deaf cat from the shelter and they love each other.

Nonfiction

A simple graphic organizer web—one center bubble and six outer bubbles—is a straightforward way to get a nonfiction summary underway. There are endless templates available, which can be useful and time-saving; kid-drawn bubbles can take a lot of time and end up filled with squished, unreadable ideas. Here are a few websites that include different templates:

- https://www.studenthandouts.com/graphic-organizers/relationships/
- https://www.studenthandouts.com/00/200003/bubble-map-graphic-organizer-worksheet.pdf

This activity needs two to four sessions.

Tiny bubbles can limit what kids will write inside them, so it may help to have just six lines radiating from the center, with a blank line at the top for writing.

Write the topic or title in the center bubble or top line. Label the far end of each radiating line with a question word: Who, What, When, Where, Why, or How. Colored pencils can help here, using a different color for each question.

One question word at a time, write key words that match it. Sometimes topics don't have information for every bubble, and that's OK. Students then go back through the words and circle or underline the one or two that they want to use from each question heading. If they're using colored pencils, have them use the same color as the question word.

Pick two of the question word headings that can go together. Use the selected words from the two headings in one sentence; kids can practice different combinations and whisper-talk until they feel ready to write. Write that sentence under the web, and X out the question word headings that you use. Repeat for two more headings, or once more for each remaining heading.

The following sample is about school. Every student should have enough information about school for the teacher to use this as the model/group activity.

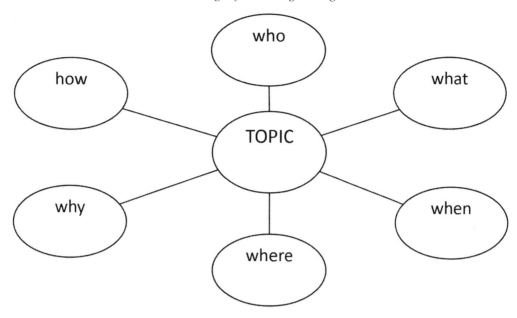

Figure 8.1. Nonfiction summary shell. Created by author.

Figure 8.2. Nonfiction summary sample. Created by author.

Sample Sentences:

- Who and What: Kids go to school and do work with teachers.
- Who and Where: Teachers and kids work together in classrooms.
- Who and Why: Kids go to school to learn stuff and get smarter.
- Who and When: Teachers and kids go to school almost every day except in the summer.
- Who and How: Kids talk and do experiments with their teachers at school.
- What and When: In the fall, winter, and spring, people go to school to learn reading and math.
- What and Where: School has classrooms and a playground so kids can work and play.
- What and Why: Kids have to learn things so they go to school to work with the teachers.

- What and How: You can do your work at school on a computer.
- What and When: During the school year, we do reading and writing work at school.

Sets of sentences that use all the bubbles complete the nonfiction summary. You may allow students to add one or two adjectives or adverbs to their sentences as a whole. Kids with higher-level skills may be able to radiate lines or bubbles from the original question word labels, to make an extended web with supporting details for the sentences or paragraphs. Each bubble can also be its own sentence for a longer, more detailed summary.

GENERAL ORGANIZATION

This strategy for organizing ideas can be adapted for almost any grade or language level, for any writing purpose. With appropriate modifications, it is effective with kindergarten through college students. It's easy to pare down or expand for almost all levels of ELs and most writers.

Dots Write

Dots Write is copyrighted by this author, with all rights reserved. It may be used only for student instruction. It may not be part of any training or professional development without express written permission from the author.

To model the process for students, the teacher will need chart paper or a large whiteboard, with markers in at least four easily discernable colors. Each student will need colored pencils or crayons in colors that roughly match the teacher's. They may choose their own colors when they work independently. They will need two clean, facing pages in their composition books. This activity will take three to five sessions.

The markers, colored pencils, or crayons are used to make dots during the process; if there are no coloring tools available, use shapes or symbols (such as circles, squares, hearts, and stars), but not numbers.

Choose a topic and write it at the top center of the left page. Students brainstorm a list of words about the topic—any words, in no particular order. Write down all suggestions. The teacher may use leading questions to help add to the list.

Use one color to draw a dot next to the first word on the brainstorm list. Help kids figure out what that word and color tell about the topic—how it looks, where it is, what it does, how it works, etc. Skip a line to note it under the list.

Go through the list one word at a time and make the same colored dot next to every word that tells the same thing about the topic. Go to the next undotted word on the list and put a different colored dot next to it. Figure out what that word and color tell about the topic. Note it under the list.

Go through the list again and make a second-color dot next to all the words that tell the same thing about the topic. Words may get more than one color dot. Go through the words with different colors until all words have been color-coded. If there are leftover words, help kids decide which colors they need, or if they should be crossed off the list.

The following sample is about recess, with a color key here instead of colored dots.

- R = red
- G = green
- B = blue
- P = purple

Recess

R outside	G run
R inside	R field
G race	R B classroom
G monkey bars	G puzzles

R playground	G P play
G talk	B grade
R gym	G games
P rules	B P friends
P fun	G read
G slide	G draw
B P playground aide	G basketball
P weather	B P class

Red - places for recess	Green - things to use at recess
Blue - people at recess	Purple - parts of recess

If the writing assignment is for multiple paragraphs, words that have more than one color can be used in the sentences that segue from one paragraph to another.

Decide with the class which color they want to write about first, then second, third, and so forth. (Students who have some independent writing skills may want to choose their own order.) On the board, make a list and have students tell you which words to add for each color:

1. Red - outside, inside, field, classroom, playground, gym
2. Blue - classroom, playground aide, friends, class, grade
3. Purple - playground aide, friends, rules, fun, weather, play, class
4. Green - basketball, slide, monkey bars, draw, read, games, talk, play, race, run, puzzles

On the right side of the double composition page, have kids make the colored dots, and next to each write only the words that they want to use. Use the words to talk through some practice sentences for each color. Have kids choose the sentence or sentences that they want to write.

Red - Sometimes recess is outside, and sometime recess is inside.

> Inside recess can be in the classroom or in the gym.
> Outside recess can be on the field next to the playground.

Blue - We have to listen to the playground aide at recess.

> During recess we can play with our friends.
> Everybody in the class goes to recess at the same time.

Purple - The playground aide makes sure that kids listen to the rules at recess.

> We have to have inside recess if the weather is too bad to go outside.
> It's fun to go out and play at recess.

Green - You can climb on the monkey bars at outside recess.

> Inside recess is nice because we can play games and read.
> You're not allowed to go down the slide backwards at recess.

Kids write their sentences on the right side of the double composition page. They may read their sentences to partners or to the class.

As a follow-up, have students transcribe their sentences to picture-story paper and draw illustrations.

POINT OF VIEW

ESOL students may understand point of view, but not have the words to show what they know, and young students, ESOL or not, are often not mature enough to understand another perspective. The following process can help, usually starting with second-graders. Use a recent story or one that kids are generally familiar with. This activity is for fiction, but for older students, it can also be used for nonfiction or fact versus opinion lessons. It will take two to four sessions.

Before writing, ask the students to raise their hands if they have ever had an argument or fight with a sibling or friend. Then have them raise their hands if it was their fault. Have them raise their hands again if it was somebody else's fault, and both hands if the other person would agree. Students can share or draw cartoons with speech bubbles about their own arguments. Tell them that when people think differently about the same thing, they have different points of view. People are different, and so are their points of view. That's OK, but it's not OK to fight about it.

Make a five-row by five-column chart with a list of main characters down the side. You probably won't need every row or column. Help students decide which describing words to write across the top. You can help with, "Was there anyone in the story who _____?"

One character at a time, go down the rows and mark each box that describes that character. Have students give reasons for their choices. Most characters won't need every box. Discuss each character's describing words. Have students ask you, "What happened?" and (you) answer from the character's Point of View.

The sample uses the fairy tale *Rumplestiltskin*, but any familiar story will work as a model.

Table 8.2.   Point of View Chart Sample

	lied	broke a promise	helped someone	made trouble
The girl/queen		x	x	
The miller	x			x
The king				x
Rumplestilskin			x	

"What happened?" asks the class. The teacher answers with appropriate feeling, facial expressions, and body language.

As the girl: I didn't say I could make straw into gold, but my father told the king that I could! If I didn't, the king was going to kill me! I needed help from that funny man. The only thing I could give him was my baby if I married the king. I didn't really think I would marry the king or have a baby!

As the miller: I said something that wasn't true, and I got my daughter into big trouble. I was just trying to feel important. I'm afraid that something bad will happen to her because of what I told the king.

As the king: I'm the king. I can do what I want. I need lots of gold, so that girl had to make some for me. If she didn't, I had to kill her for cheating the king. If she did, I would marry her so I could get richer and richer.

As Rumplestiltskin: I saved that girl's life three times! I helped her! I made gold for the king! She gave me some jewelry, then she promised me a real baby. She was crying, so I gave her a chance to keep the baby. But she cheated!

Have students use their composition books or picture-story paper folded into two columns. Each student may choose any two characters from the story and write their names, one at the top of each column. Students will draw the characters they choose, each with a speech or thought bubble about their part in the story.

Students will write one sentence under each picture, with sentence starters if needed.

The girl was crying because _____.

Rumplestilskin was mad because _____.

Have students read their character's bubbles (in character) and sentences to the class. You can end by talking about who the students think is "right" or what was or wasn't fair.

THE KID PIECE OF THE WRITING PUZZLE

Kids want to talk about themselves and people they know and generally to figure out their places in the big picture. As complicated and difficult as writing may feel, it helps kids explore and find where they fit in the school world. For ESOL and young learners, the language skills at hand are generally egocentric, so writing assignments should start in the "me space." There are a few ideas here to help get things started, but anything that has a common experience or feeling to it will usually work. With these kids, writing starts by talking.

- Write letters to friends, family, classmates, incoming classes, school staff, and authors.
- Likes and Dislikes – animals, foods, seasons, TV shows, school activities, and so on—with reasons
- A trip (school or family)
- Would you/wouldn't you (do something scary, share a favorite toy, tell on a friend, etc.)
- Write alternate endings/draw cartoon panels for familiar stories.
- Complete a bar graph about skills or strengths. Talk and then write to describe part/s of it or how it compares to a classmate's (see Appendix D, The Great Graph).
- Write a name-acrostic poem and describe part/s of it.
- Show and Tell, but write about someone else's presentation (use a capture sheet to help).
- Star of the Week presentation with students writing recaps (use a capture sheet to help).
- A Stuffed Animal Journal – A stuffed animal with a cute journal travels home in its own small backpack or bag. The student recounts their evening or weekend together and takes it all back to school to share and pass on to the next student.

Six-Word Memoirs

This is just what it sounds like! The writer uses only six words in a simple sentence or two to convey the essence of something personal. Kids can start with or add illustrations about a myriad of possible topics. The Six-Word Memoirs website (https://www.sixwordmemoirs.com/) has books, contests, themes, examples and other fun stuff to help teachers and kids make good use of this strategy.

OWL Purdue Online Writing Lab

This online site provides resources to ESOL teachers and students: https://owl.english.purdue.edu/owl/resource/678/01/.

Maryland Public Television

Maryland Public Television's homepage has an inclusive set of graphic organizers to download, print, and use for free: http://www.thinkport.org/graphic-organizers.html.
They include:

- Compare/Contrast – for similarities and differences between characters, situations, concepts, settings, and so on
- Concept Map – to organize main ideas and supporting details
- Cornell Note-Taking – to organize nonfiction information
- Fishbone – for cause-and-effect details and events
- Hypothesizing – to help identify the three main parts of a hypothesis
- K-W-L or K-W-H-L (**K**now - **W**ant to know - **H**ow I learned - **L**earned) – to review and provide background information before introducing new material, then to add the new information
- Plot Diagram – to diagram and outline story elements
- Sequence of Events Chart – to put events in chronological order
- Spider Map – to organize a number of ideas with their supporting details
- SQ3R (Survey, Question, Read, Recite, Review) - to help sort and reinforce nonfiction
- Story Map – to organize the story structure of fiction
- Storyboard – to illustrate main events

- Timeline – to organize main events in chronological order
- Tree – to connect different ideas and details, especially with limited background knowledge
- Venn Diagram – to compare and contrast different ideas or elements
- W's Organizer – to organize the five main "wh" questions - who, what , when, where, why
- Web – to develop a frame for key ideas
- Website Profiler – to determine the validity and value of an online site
- Wheel and Spoke – to develop a framework for concepts

Most of these graphic organizers are provided in Word documents, and have the "Enable Editing" button so teachers and students can change them as needed.

KEY TAKEAWAYS

- Writing is complicated and intimidating for many ESOL students and young kids.
- It takes a long time to master academic writing.
- Writing is a process that should start with talking, especially for ELs and little kids.
- Talk and read through every part of the process.
- It's OK to change your mind during the writing process.
- Simple step-by-step procedures help kids get started and stay on track.
- Summaries don't need many details, mostly just key words.
- Colors, graphic organizers, and capture sheets help students organize, remember, and use their ideas.
- Graphic organizers can save time and help with legibility.
- It's OK to have a different point of view.
- There are lots of personal connections or common experiences for kids to write about.

NINE

What's the Problem?

ELs make mistakes. The kind and frequency of the mistakes can help teachers understand what, if anything, is holding up language mastery. The long-range goal of correct language use will progress through

- recognition of errors,
- correction with help,
- correction with prompting,
- self-correction in isolation, and
- self-correction in context.

If a student can't get to self-correction, there may be a more general problem in his or her learning profile.

There's a team of skilled professionals at school who are assets to classroom teachers with struggling students. A collaborative approach as early as possible can clear a lot of stumbling stones from the EL student's path. The school history of Manny, below, is an excellent example of how teamwork with counselors, school psychologists, administration, reading specialists, and special educators could have helped monitor and identify problems and kept them from snowballing.

ESOL AND SPECIAL NEEDS

For years there was an unfortunate assumption in many schools that every academic stumble from an ESOL student was part of the language-acquisition process. Another misunderstanding among ESOL families was that an English-language-learning program was the same as special education. Each of these mindsets created confusion and problems for ESOL students, their families, and their teachers. They caused ESOL parents to decline much-needed English instruction for their students, with the long-term effect that many kids never got the basic language skills necessary for them to work as well as they could think. They also delayed or eliminated help that some ESOL students needed early in their learning.

This chapter will illustrate that ESOL and special education are not the same and are not mutually exclusive. It will describe common language-acquisition errors that kids and teachers need to work on, but not worry about. It will also describe patterns or language problems that are not typical and that warrant other, non-ESOL help and suggest ways to tease out which is which. The following example sounds extreme but is all too typical.

Manny came to the United States from Central America when he was seven years old, after failing first grade in his home country. The family said that he had been living with an older sister, but moved to the United States to be with his mother and stepfather. He was much younger than the older siblings already here. The family also said that the older sister in the home country was slow to learn and that she had had a very difficult time in school, so did not attend for long.

At age fifteen, Manny was in eighth grade, and did not read or write even though he could clearly understand and speak English. He came to school, but hung out with a troublesome crowd, did no work, and had been suspended a few times for fighting. Over the years in various schools, several of his teachers had recommended that he be considered for educational evaluation. They never got past the initial referral; it always came back, "He's ESOL." Early in his US school history, that was an understandable response. But after eight years in English-speaking American schools, an English-speaking student who still cannot read or write is not struggling with acquisition.

Miss Rogers was new to the building to set up a different ESOL program and took Manny's enormous file to the principal during the first week of school. The principal agreed that Manny had been overlooked because of his ESOL status, and pushed through a recommendation for screening. Miss Rogers and Manny worked well together, and he eventually told her about a medical issue that embarrassed him and prompted some of his fights. The administrator allowed Miss Rogers to contact the public health nurse assigned to the school, who in turn contacted Manny's family. The nurse walked them through the process of getting the necessary referrals for Manny to see a specialist and get the medicine he needed. The positive change was remarkable in how he felt and presented himself, if not in how he learned.

Manny's evaluations came back with the expected results that he had significant specific learning disabilities and was on the low end of the general intelligence bell curve. He turned sixteen before the end of his eighth-grade school year, and, that summer, he officially left school.

If ESOL needs had not been misinterpreted and used to excuse his lack of progress, Manny would have been screened well before he left elementary school, would likely have had learning supports for some school success, and would have been far less likely to drop out. A team approach, with observations, instruction, and feedback from a spectrum of specialists, would have helped save energy, angst, time, effort, and this student's academic story.

ESOL

Language mistakes by ELs generally follow a pattern similar to the mistakes of native English speakers when they are first learning to talk. Vocabulary is limited, pronunciations can be off, and grammar rules are generalized and somewhat inaccurate.

- The kid at the end of the line is the "line backer."
- "Brother" is "bruvver" or "brudder."
- "Ate" is "eated."
- "My" or "mine" is "mines."

Over time and with practice, these errors largely vanish. Language learning requires a lot of mental energy, attention, and effort, so when kids are acquiring new language, they place previously mastered skills on the back burner while they figure out the new stuff. It looks like they've forgotten or neglected what seemed to be solid. When learners feel secure about the new skills, they combine them with already-learned material and create a higher platform for the next set of language material.

They master A.
They start B, so put A away.
They master B, get A out, and create AB.
They master AB.
They start C, so put AB away.
They master C, so get AB out and create ABC.
And so on.

ESOL students that are making mistakes, but are generally following this pattern, are on the right track. They and their teachers will need to continue to practice and refine their language work, but mistakes like this are not cause for concern.

Common Errors (Don't Worry)

ESOL students infer general rules of grammar and pronunciation as they hear new structures and feel their way through the new language. The generalizations are modified over time. If students don't move away from these general rules or common errors, it can be a red flag that something is wrong with their process. Teachers can intuit when something isn't going right for their students and check with ESOL or other specialists about ELs who seem stalled. They can also intuit when the kid is going along at a reasonable pace and will continue to improve.

Prepositions

There are innumerable idioms and phrases with English prepositions. Mistakes with prepositions are typical and don't usually obscure meaning.

- "at my birthday" instead of "on my birthday"
- "in my house" instead of "at home"
- "in the bus" instead of "on the bus"

Pronunciation

Some sounds are hard for ELs whose home languages do not use the same speaking muscles as English. The younger an EL is, the easier it will be for him or her to correctly form the new sounds. ELs who don't enunciate in their home language will follow a lax pronunciation pattern in English and make the speaker hard to understand. They need specific, continued attention. They should raise eyebrows only if they don't respond to continued support.

- d/f/s/t/v for th - baffroom for bathroom, bruvver/brudder for brother, duh for the
- dz for j - dzump for jump
- sh for s - yesh for yes
- sh for ch - share for chair, shocolate for chocolate
- s for x - bos for box, essept for except
- es for s - estay for stay
- j or l for y - jes for yes, joo for you, jello/lellow for yellow
- v for w - vee for we
- b for v - berry for very
- n for m - suntine for sometimes
- dropped ending sounds - ha' for has or have, fi'e for five
- dropped contractions - can' for can't, dozen for doesn't
- in' for ing - workin', eatin', playin'

ELs will spell what they speak, so mispronunciations carry over from speaking into writing. Polishing the rough edges of oral language improves written language and helps provide a better academic picture of the EL.

Past Tense

Did - ELs usually understand the word "did" in past tense questions ("Did you wash your hands?"), but have trouble taking it out of the answer. They often use the past tense "did" as well as the past tense of the main verb, as in "Yes, I did washed my hands." This is a common mistake and can be corrected by reinforcing that "did" is part of the verb and only one part has to be in past tense.

"ed" - The suffix "ed" that marks a verb as past tense has two pronunciations:

/d/ as in smiled, studied, pulled

/t/ as in cooked, walked, pushed

ELs sometimes emphasize or add the "ed" suffix as "did," as in "walkdid" or "heardid" until they have enough practice with regular and irregular past tense and using words that have the /d/ and /t/ endings. This is a generalization of the past tense "rule," like other general grammar rules inferred by early talkers. Correct use and exceptions come with practice.

Question/Answer Word Order

Word order for questions and answers differs from language to language. To simplify things, ESOL students will often just make a statement with a rise in tone at the end, as in "I can have snack?" Model the correct way to ask, "May I please have a snack?" and have them repeat it. When ESOL students use the "wh" words in questions, they often make a statement with a "wh" work stuck at the beginning, as in "When I can go?" After they learn the correct order of question word + verb, as in "Where is the dog?" they still have trouble unwinding the word order for answers to some "wh" questions.

> Question: Where is the dog?
> Answer: I don't know where is the dog.
> Question: Who the helper is today?
> Answer: I know who is the helper today.
> Question: What day is it?
> Answer: I don't know what day is it.

This can be a lingering detail for ELs, but it doesn't indicate a serious problem.

Literal Translations That Just Need Practice

- For we could (in response to "why?") - so we can *(Get in the line for we could go to recess.)*
- Throw - throw away *(I can throw my lunch tray?)*
- Not me, too - me neither *(I can' hear the teacher. Not me, too.)*

Kids will generally move through these typical errors at a fairly predictable rate. They're part of the process for developing correct English. If, however, an EL student gets stuck or progress stalls, it's worth taking a closer look for what else might be going on.

Uncommon Errors (It's Time to Worry)

The ESOL picture is complicated, and in turn can complicate general learning and the decisions about whether or not a student needs an evaluation. There are a lot of factors to look at when deciding if an EL student warrants a screening for special education support.

Time in Country

Kids new to the country, who are still adjusting, will often transfer a lot of learning energy to social-emotional energy. They may be acting out, unresponsive, inattentive, inappropriate, or any other uh-oh adjective. It may be a quick transition, but it could also take most of the school year. Remember Rico, the little boy from Chile, in chapter 1?

If a student comes into the US school with a history of special education or learning difficulties from the home country, it makes sense to address the problems immediately. (See Manny's story in this chapter.) If there is no history, it behooves the school to allow the student as much time and space as is reasonable. Raise the red flag if necessary, of course; precise documentation is a federal mandate, adds to an accurate educational history, protects the school, and best serves the student in the long run. Provide supports that don't require IEPs. They may include an academic coach, school tutor, counselor visits, and/or family meetings. (As noted in chapter 2, use discretion when contacting parents or guardians about their student's negative behaviors or problems at school.) Reasonable accommodations are allowed by virtue of the student's ESOL status.

The following is an extreme example of a We Need More Time! situation.

Vietnamese-speaking NEP identical twin boys came into Kindergarten. They were new to the area, and had recently moved from the other side of the country to live with their father and his extended family. From the very beginning, they fell way outside the norms—they had never been to school, were mute except with each other, were very undersized, did not acknowledge their classmates or the teachers, had to be within arm's reach of each other, would not engage even in independent center activities, and moved in an unusually stiff way.

It took Miss Rogers and the Kindergarten teacher about half a minute to start keeping records on these brothers. Their skinny cumulative folders provided no insights. There was an administrator meeting almost immediately with the father to suggest that the boys be placed in a half-day pre-K class, but he proved to be as inflexible about school as his sons.

By the end of Kindergarten, it was obvious that the twins could understand math and read, as long as they worked alone. Their receptive skills were well underway, but they used almost no productive language except with each other. They had normal hearing and vision checks but their low engagement with teachers and classmates made them appear significantly impaired. After first grade, the principal was finally able to administratively place the boys in separate classrooms, but every teacher through grade 3 struggled with how to work with them. Their ESOL scores flatlined from year to year because they wouldn't respond to most of the test items on the proficiency assessments.

Early in the boys' second-grade year, Miss Rogers found them a male Vietnamese transition counselor who could come to the school and work with the twins every week. In two school years, he got them to respond when spoken to and to at least start their written assignments. He also got the father to tell what had happened to the boys before they came to Kindergarten. It was a terrible story and an emotional history that weighted two tiny kids with a burden they could never shed by themselves.

Things started to get a little easier for the boys when the family accepted that the school could and would help and to decline help would put the brothers further and further behind their classmates. There was every indication that the twins were easily smart enough to do the work, but also every indication that something was seriously wrong. If the school had not been attuned to the vagaries of ESOL kids' lives, the twins would have found themselves in an academic setting outside general education. It would have been extremely limiting and a disservice to them. As the two of them started to emerge, it got easier to tell them apart because teachers had a much better sense of how smart and funny each one was, and could see them as individual personalities. They even started to respond to offers of friendship from their classmates.

There was another must-be-patient situation with Kindergarten twins in the same building the year the twin boys were in first grade. This was a set of fraternal twin girls from Romania. The parents and middle-school siblings were bilingual; they spoke English very well, and used their native language at home.

Angelika was the more extroverted sister. Catina was very shy and relied on Angelika to manage things for her. The girls came through the international admissions office and took the English placement test there. Angelika scored a 4.7 out of 5 overall; Catina scored a zero. The principal asked Miss Rogers to do an informal language assessment with Catina, but Catina had a meltdown when she realized she'd have to leave the classroom without Angelika. The same thing happened the second time Miss Rogers went to see Catina.

There was no value to provoking hysteria in the Kindergarten room, so the ESOL teacher went to Plan B, with the principal's approval. Catina seemed to qualify for ESOL services, but it was obvious that she wasn't going anywhere—like the ESOL room—without Angelika. Given her sister's high scores and the family background, it was also unlikely that her zero was accurate.

The family agreed that Catina's low score wasn't a true picture, and that she had been too overwhelmed by the move to the United States to do what the placement test asked. They signed the waiver of services letter, with the understanding that it would be revisited later in the school year. By then, Catina agreed to go with Miss Rogers "just one time" to practice English. "Willing" might be too strong a word, but she was "compliant" in taking the annual proficiency test. Catina sailed through and earned scores that didn't require ESOL support. She had had the skills, she just had to settle in so she could focus on using them.

Is the Student in an ESOL Program?

Is the student part of a small or specialized group with ESOL support or instruction? If so, how long has the student been there?

Young kids through grade 1, and often grade 2, haven't had enough practice with English and/or can just be immature and not "there" yet. There's usually not enough data, anecdotal records, or work samples to make a case for screening until a student has been at school, in an ESOL program, for at least two years. It helps to start documenting problems as soon as the teacher/s suspect something.

If a student has been receiving regular ESOL support for at least one school year, preferably two, but is not keeping up with students in the same grade and/or ESOL group, it's time to start looking for impediments.

The most straightforward issues to address are physically oriented: food, clothing, sleep, vision, and hearing. If the school doesn't have a vision and hearing screening scheduled within a good time frame, check with the public health nurse assigned to the school to set something up with the parents. If glasses or an ear rinse is all that's needed, school life could improve immediately. If a family can't afford the screening services or glasses, the school system usually has programs available through public health or the ESOL Department. The family may be aware that their student has a problem, but not have sufficient English, finances, or know-how to take care of it.

Three ESOL sisters across three consecutive lower grades all struggled with academic work. They failed their preliminary and follow-up vision tests at school, and the parents were notified, but there was no response. The school nurse contacted the mother and found out that the family could not afford three pairs of glasses. The nurse arranged vouchers with a big-box store and all the girls had glasses within a couple of weeks.

Unfortunately, during frequent Battles of the Siblings, their go-to offense was to grab and break each other's glasses. A nearby optometrist donated repairs, but that had reasonable limits, especially for fixes that were not simple.

Miss Rogers had a serious sit-down with the girls and described her heartfelt sadness and disappointment that during Shared Reading, the girls couldn't have their turns because they didn't have their glasses and wouldn't be able to see the words. She also told them that she couldn't get the glasses fixed anymore. It struck a chord, and the girls pinky-promised to keep their hands off the others' glasses (most of the time).

A Kindergarten student who was ready and willing to be part of school activities was oddly unresponsive when she wasn't close to the teacher. Even in the small, quiet ESOL setting, she seemed to be unclear about what was going on. Her speaking skills weren't developing, and she ignored oral directions. The Kindergarten teacher saw the same behaviors, so Miss Rogers contacted the school nurse, who contacted the family. She got a referral to a hearing specialist, whom the family went to immediately. The student's ears were full of hard, dense wax. Once she was treated, her hearing was clear, language skills took off, and she was a quick, happy English Learner.

Check for nutritional or sleep needs, too. Kids can't concentrate if all their energy is used up thinking about food or trying to stay awake. Remember the eight-year-old patriarch, Marco, who even the dog listened to in chapter 1? If students are on the Free and Reduced Meals (FARM) program, make sure they get their breakfast and lunch every day. Kids on the FARM program who get to school late will often skip breakfast, but teachers must insist as much as possible that they get their food and eat it. If the kids can't eat in the cafeteria or the classroom, check with the counselor, ESOL teacher, or other staffer whose space might be available during homeroom. It will only take a few minutes (since they're not overchatting with FARM friends instead of eating) but the positive effect will be significant.

Do an Academic History

Look at the student's classroom records to find a pattern of difficulties. Is it mostly math, or mostly reading or writing? What do the report card comments say? Get input from as many current and former teachers as possible. What have they seen the student struggle with?

Talk to the parent or guardian about problems they see in the home language. Was the student a late talker, or does the student have pronunciation or comprehension problems in the home language? Did anyone else in the family have the same struggles? Find out how the student handles homework, the kinds of things the student likes to do in his or her free time, and the kinds of activities the student avoids (e.g., a student with writing problems will probably hide or put off written homework and not like fine-motor activities like Legos.) Students who have memory issues and/or attention problems will forget the homework, forget the materials, forget where their backpack is, forget that they left the kitchen table to find their backpack, and then disappear. When disgorged from their bedroom, they will say, "Why are you so mad?"

Ask ESOL students if there's anything that is hard for them. Kids know what they're not good at. For example, when a stellar reading student in a disheartening, eternal struggle with math was asked, "What part is hard for you?" She hollered, "THE NUMBERS!" Her brother was an intuitive and clever scientist, but failed every science test. When the errors were analyzed, his science answers were 100 percent correct, but the calculations for scientific formulas were 100 percent wrong. Both kids were found to have dyscalculia.

Compare language proficiency scores across the academic years. Language proficiency tests are not meant to be diagnostic and cannot stand alone in figuring out what's going on or not going on with ESOL kids. They are, however, a significant part of the big picture for ESOL kids. They contribute important details about where the student is and isn't making strides.

Most assessments provide graphics of scores for students who take the annual test. Compare the numbers or scales across the years of testing. Look for one (or some) that are significantly behind the others or that haven't moved much. If there's a disproportionate gap with the same domain/s, that's a good indicator that something other than ESOL is interfering with the student's learning. It's unusual for a student to make even progress across the domains, so expect discrepancies within 1–1.5 levels of each other. See Appendix E: Comparing Proficiency Levels Over Time.

Here's another example: A smart, cooperative third-grade ESOL student who was making progress in reading did poorly on quizzes and tests. She had EL accommodations that included a read-to, and her productive work was very good. Her weakness with assessments was puzzling until her K, grade 1, and grade 2 ESOL proficiency assessments were analyzed as a whole. They showed an increasing gap between Listening and the other three major domains. She was found to have an auditory processing disability; the read-to accommodation was actually making the work harder for her.

Compare ESOL progress with students in the same grade who entered ESOL at the same time at roughly the same level. If the student is being outpaced by the group in general, take a closer look. That said, remember to consider the literacy and schooling levels at home.

Jay was an articulate, curious, and well-informed fourth-grader. His family ran a successful bilingual business and was supportive, active, and engaged. But Jay was just not making progress with reading and writing, although he could talk about anything and had excellent auditory memory.

Classmates that had entered ESOL with him in Kindergarten had all exited. For two years before Miss Rogers set up a new ESOL program, Jay had been recommended in grades 2 and 3 for screening, but was declined because he was ESOL. His Listening and Speaking domains were well past Exit levels, but the Reading and Writing stayed quite low.

When he was finally evaluated, he was found to have significant disabilities in those areas. His parents signed an ESOL waiver letter to create room in his schedule for special education resource. The classroom, ESOL, and resource teachers conferred, and with different approaches and strategies through special education, he was able to exit ESOL at the end of fifth grade. English language classes had been giving him tools he didn't know how to use; special education taught him how to use the tools he had.

See Appendix F: Comparing Proficiency Scores Within a Group.

Work Samples

The composition books that ELs use in ESOL class are an excellent way to show progress, or lack of progress, over time. They can illustrate uncommon, repeated errors from a small-group setting. The classroom teacher can provide work samples from whole-class or independent centers. Together, they can support the need to investigate the source of continuing mistakes not common to ESOL or the grade level.

A second-grade teacher and Miss Rogers were trying to decide if a particular ESOL student's writing problem warranted closer inspection, or if being an immature writer was part of his general "whatever" persona and/or his language level. Farzaad's writing was very slow, letters were poorly formed and placed (but legible), and spelling was inconsistent. He stopped writing and put a period at the end of every line, even if the sentence wasn't finished. Overall, he wrote at a very early level, not uncommon among ELs in the primary grades.

Miss Rogers happened to give his class an assignment to write a sentence using a conjunction (resulting in a longer-than-usual sentence). Farzaad talked through his sentence and got the thumbs up to do the writing and illustration on the picture-story paper. He drew his modern-art picture and then started the sentence on the far left side of the top line, as expected. When he got to the far right side of the paper, though, he flipped it over sideways, and continued writing with backwards letters, right to left.

Miss Rogers decided to call a meeting with the second-grade teacher.

Articulation

Mispronunciations are part of the ESOL package, but there are times when intervention is warranted. Listen for which letter sounds are consistently wrong and watch students' mouths as they talk. Kids will sometimes tell you that they need help.

A third-grade girl once asked Miss Rogers, "What's the gwade when they teach you the 'ow' sound?" (What's the grade when they teach you the "r" sound?) It was an isolated sound and didn't warrant a long trip through the IEP maze, so Miss Rogers asked the speech therapist to teach her how to teach the student the way to use her tongue, teeth, and lips to make the sound accurately.

An Intermediate-ESOL Kindergarten boy, who was predisposed not to break a sweat, sounded like a "lazy" talker—his speech was low, fast, and garbled. His speech improved a little in quantity, but not quality, through first and into second grade. Just as it was time to consider a speech and language evaluation, Miss Rogers overheard a conversation between him and another student. Henri said something about the toys they were using, and the other boy said, "What?" Henri repeated himself, as did the other boy. Henri sighed and said under his breath, "Nobody understands me when I talk."

The speech specialist did an informal observation and recognized that the student was tongue-tied. (The frenulum is the skin that attaches the bottom of the tongue to the floor of the mouth. If the frenulum is ill-placed or too short to be flexible for all speech sounds, the speaker is often unintelligible.) The speech specialist recommended the student for a speech screening, explained the problem and the small procedure to remedy it to the parents, and provided speech services to Henri after the frenulum was corrected. Within a year, although he was still generally lethargic about school work, he spoke clearly.

Vincent was alert and happy in his Kindergarten classroom and in ESOL; he smiled a lot and spoke very little. He was a beginner, so his silence wasn't worrisome. When he did start to speak, however, he had a significant stammer. The front end of what he was saying started out with repeated and prolonged sounds and the rest followed in a loud gasping rush. He was met with "He's stalling" on the first referral for evaluation in first grade. "He's ESOL" was the response on the next referral in second grade, but Miss Rogers prevailed by pointing out that if it was normal ESOL speech, all ESOL kids would stammer.

His classroom teacher provided anecdotal records, and his family confirmed that he used the same speech pattern in the home language. They thought it was just anxiety about holding the floor to be heard, and they were partly right. The speech evaluation showed that Vincent needed to learn breath and volume control, and to pace his words from start to finish. ESOL probably played a part in his stammer, but it was neither the cause nor the solution.

Not in an ESOL Program?

If a student is not in an ESOL program, there is very little an ESOL teacher can do besides consult with other teachers who are concerned about an ESOL-eligible or exited student. It is the family's right to decline ESOL services but doing so removes supports for the student. A classroom teacher, ESOL teacher, or administrator may meet with the family decision-maker/s and point out the values of targeted English language instruction, and how it can shore up a struggling student to keep the student from falling further behind. If the family won't change their minds, though, the ESOL specialist is out of the picture as a teacher-of-record or active participant in planning for the student.

Classroom teachers can work with the ESOL teacher for materials, strategies, or insights into what's going on with EL students who aren't getting the language instruction they need. It will be harder to support the need for special education screening, as the argument of limited English proficiency won't have rebuttal. As always, document, document, document.

KEY TAKEAWAYS

- ESOL mistakes follow patterns that eventually recede.
- Common ESOL errors are not usually cause for alarm.
- ESOL students learn to self-correct their language mistakes.
- Some EL learning problems can be partially resolved by meeting physical needs like health care, food, and sleep.
- English acquisition can be troublesome but is neither the cause of nor the solution to learning disabilities or other special education needs.
- English proficiency tests can provide insights into slow or stalled academic progress for ESOL kids.
- Referrals for screening of ESOL students usually require more extensive data, anecdotal records, and work samples than non-ESOL student referrals.
- Articulation problems that are outside the norm for learning to make English sounds, and that don't resolve over time, need attention from a speech and language specialist.
- If a learning behavior or problem is outside the norm for non-ESOL students, it is probably outside the norm for ESOL students.
- "It's an ESOL problem" holds true in the referral process only if it applies to almost all of the EL population and most of the ELs are having the same problem.
- Check domains on the proficiency tests over time to look for a pattern of weakness in particular areas.
- Compare a worrisome EL's general progress to that of other ELs who entered the program at roughly the same time and/or at the same proficiency levels.
- An ESOL specialist will be of limited help to an EL who is not part of the formal ESOL program.
- Document, document, document.

TEN

What Teachers and Kids Say

The following words of wisdom are from elementary teachers and ESOL students who have been successful in their classrooms.

TEACHERS

Dawn E. Audibert — Pre-K–1

1. Provide *lots* of visuals and props, including thematic puppets, jewelry, or clothes that go with the unit and will hold the kids' attention.
2. Move to songs and actions. Lots of Total Physical Response (TPR) keeps the learning vibrant.
3. Make up dances that go with the songs available on SMART Boards.
4. Always use a combination of phonics and whole language.
5. Integrate shared experience writing.
6. Make everything as multisensory as possible; the more senses are involved, the more vibrant it will be and the more it will lead to better learning.
7. Not everything is bells and whistles. Include calm, quiet learning and work times.
8. Study buddies — find ESOL and non-ESOL kids that have something in common (kids wearing basketball shirts, matching lunchboxes, older or younger siblings) and have them work together. The ESOL student will have a role model for age-appropriate language and will feel safe talking to another little person who will be a friend. The friend widens the social circle for the ESOL student, who then feels like part of the class and is more ready to raise his or her hand.
9. Don't abandon previously learned skills. Go back periodically to check that kids remember what they did several weeks ago.
10. Use mnemonic devices like this to help kids remember how to spell "because": *Bunnies eat carrots and usually see everything.*

Leslie Shear — Kindergarten

I use many props, costumes, puppets, and body language. What is natural for teaching five-year-olds happens to be best practices for teaching ESOL students as well. Also, there is no better way to teach young children than by using music. K teachers use songs to teach every subject and make it fun. It works for ESOL students, too!

Melissa Ruben — Grade 1

- Time management: In terms of ESOL students and managing time met with them, *sticky notes* are key! I keep them all over, and a pad of them nearby at all times. For reading groups, I keep a sticky note with times that students are pulled out so that I remember not to meet with them or have them start a brand new task at that time. I know other teachers use calendars, outlook alerts, and so forth, but I have found that sticky notes are most helpful because when things pop up (for example, ESOL testing or PARCC so the ESOL teacher won't be meeting with them that day), I can always make new ones, adjust, and so on.

- Self-care: In terms of being a new teacher in general, make sure that you make time for yourself. Set a time to arrive/leave school every day and stick to it. Schedule gym classes or activities after school so you are forced to leave, and not stay until it's bed time.
- Groups: Provide all the visual cues and tools you give to ESOL students in the classroom in reading groups as well. In fact, introduce them there first and let them try them out, then let them take them with them to their desks for independent work.

   Be strategic about center groups. For students who have a hard time speaking English, it can be frustrating to be paired with all English speakers who aren't as empathetic. Try to put the "helpers" in the groups with ESOL students so that they can be supportive and kind to the students as they rotate through independent work.
- Technology: When possible, use technology (Google Translate, Google Images, etc.) to help support lessons for students who do not speak English as a first language.
- Parent/Student relationships: When possible, make an effort to show you are trying to accommodate their needs. Use Google Translate or find translated versions of worksheets or flyers that go home. Learn some basic words from the language that they speak and use them in the classroom.

I have a recent example of a student who is not in my class, but is in another first-grade class. When he first got to our school, he spoke little to no English (only Spanish). When I saw him in the hallway, I would make an effort to say hello, using his name, in Spanish. I don't know that much Spanish, but my high-school classes came back to me quickly and I used what little Spanish I did know in conversation with him, and for words I did not know, I looked them up. This would always put a smile on his face, and he still to this day comes by my classroom every day just to say "Hi Ms. Ruben!" Showing an interest in him and making a moderate effort to learn and use his language meant so much to him, and I am sure he went home and told his parents as well.

Amanda Zammillo—Grades 1–2 and Reading

- Use songs, vocabulary cards, visuals, and sentence starters.
- Front-load vocabulary and incorporate TPR using hand/body to learn new vocabulary.
- Use Think-Pair-Share.

Nancy Craig—Grade 2

My newcomer used the computer program Starfall.com a lot. It reinforced letters and words, had stories he could listen to, and allowed him to hear the language and see pictures. I also paired him up with a buddy—he seemed to learn a lot about the schedule and what to do during the day.

I made picture and color cards with the word on the card to go with the picture.

I also had him keep a journal. I would write sentences and he would read and illustrate ("The red ball is big"). The journal gave him something that he could read—it was his book, if you will.

We played matching games with the letters and words written on cards. He would also say the letter or word as he matched it.

He also enjoyed buddy reading—listening to a buddy read to him.

Robb Wainwright—Grades 1–3 and Reading

Relationships are the most important way to help students engage best in their learning. Talking to ESOL students is vitally important in helping them understand that their voice is as important as all the other voices in the classroom. As ESOL students feel valued they become less focused on how differently they speak, read, write, or learn.

After talking to a student, to better understand what they want to articulate, I will tell the student, "Say it this way: ____." Sometimes my colleagues think this is too abrupt an approach. I think this structure and good modeling is beneficial for ESOL students for many reasons: They are engaged in conversation, they are expressing their thoughts, they hear a proper model of how to express their thinking, and their confidence improves because they are able to communicate clearly with their peers and teachers.

A combination of focused instruction outside of the classroom with integrated support within the classroom works best. Outside support should address specific skills that the classroom instruction does not address. The integrated support is equally important as it helps ESOLers function more fluidly within the classroom.

At times, other non-ESOL students can become interested and then take on a role of supporting their ESOL peers, creating the collaborative environment where all students work best.

The ESOL and classroom teacher communicate on a regular basis so that the curriculum of each person can be braided with the other. This allows ESOL students to be supported within the same lesson as their peers, allowing them to become a better part of the community.

Classroom teachers can benefit from learning ESOL strategies they can implement on their own, increasing the amount of support ESOL students receive. These strategies often work well with all learners, positively impacting all the students and helping ESOL students feel less alienated or isolated.

ESOL teachers benefit as they infuse their strategies and lessons around the content/purpose of the classroom curriculum. Students often benefit from the common language and expectations of both professionals and settings.

Erica Valenstein—Grades 2 and 4

- Question and Thought journal to share with the teacher
- picture writing
- new-word dictionary/book (kids create their own new word book as they learn new words)
- group chats before writing anything to give them an opportunity to test out the new words/vocabulary
- have the kids create their own word bank before writing

Jennifer Shin Ahn—Grades 3, 4, and 5

- Provide visuals and models for everything. Providing visuals for challenging concepts is helpful for all students. Models help the students to understand what their completed assignment will look like.
- Speak clearly and slowly so that they are able to follow the directions being given or the concepts being taught.
- Provide students with additional wait time. It may take longer for ESOL students to orally formulate their responses.
- Allow students to work with other students in groups. When students have the opportunity to learn in groups, they are more engaged, and group work provides students the time to practice their language with their peers.
- Create word walls with high-frequency words arranged alphabetically.
- Provide sentence starters/language frames when completing written work. Provide opportunities for the students to draw about their thinking.
- Provide word boxes to help students with their vocabulary.
- Preview vocabulary with pictures prior to reading a text.
- Learn about the culture of the student. This helps the teacher to form a closer relationship with the student.
- Have an interpreter for meetings if parents do not speak English. This will help the teacher to form a positive relationship with the family.

Linda Jordan—Grades 3 and 5

I use lots of easy sayings:

- "If you can dream it, you can do it."
- "What do you see . . . what do you notice?"
- "Act as if"

I also use "bucket" statements. If you fill someone's bucket with kindness, cheerfulness, and friendliness, you get those things also.

I use gentle humor. Individual importance and our classroom community are important to make everyone feel valued and safe.

Each day I teach everyone a "big" word and their homework is to use it once at home. The best thing, though, is when they find some of the words in books. It's a great way to get them to read carefully.

Deborah Becker—English Language Development Teacher Coach

Students need to talk about academic content for these reasons:

- to process the content and the vocabulary to develop their understanding,
- to engage and make connections that help students remember the information, and
- to develop the language they need to express their understanding (in speaking or writing).

This is essential.

INPUT FROM KIDS (WITH SOME GRAMMAR CORRECTIONS)

Grade 1

- She tells us all about it, especially in math with times.
- She lets me talk to my friends for help.
- She tells me again.
- She puts pictures up on the SMART Board.
- She shows what it looks like and shows what she did so we can see how we do it.
- She writes the directions on the board and she reads them.
- She tells me things extra times.
- She repeats the words over again cuz they're kinda long.
- She reads it over again.
- She tells us to find the word in the Word Book if you don't know it. She helps me spell a word by saying yes or no when I say a letter.
- She gives us Golden Noodle time to get your body moving.
- She lets me read Arthur books.

Grade 2

- She underlines the hard words.
- She helps you spell.
- She gives us clues and how to do it.
- She helps me. She writes English for me to copy.
- She gives me sentence starters.
- She gives us graphic organizers.
- She waits for me to think about it.
- She lets me talk to her by myself for help.
- She checks my work.
- She writes stuff for me to copy. She lets me draw pictures first for Book Writing.
- She uses a nice voice.

Grades 3–5

- My teacher lets me use a voice-to-text feature to help me write.
- Defines words when I don't know the meaning.
- He speaks slowly.
- My teacher explained everything and she always asked us if we have any questions. Other kids said their teachers do not explain but my teacher really takes time explaining everything.
- I liked when we made things. I remember how we made the clay snowmen. I liked when we collaborated in groups in my class.
- I didn't have an accent, but I didn't like to talk. Then two Spanish kids came to my class and my teacher let us work together. I helped them and it helped me come out of my shell.
- Scribing, breaks down words.
- Help me with pronouncing words in English by repeating what they say.
- They explain multiple meanings of words so I understand how to use them.
- They explain math again and again, to help me understand the question.
- They break down math questions and ask the same question in different ways with different words I might understand better.
- Breaks down words with prefix and suffix to help me understand the meaning
- When they ask a question they will give me a simple version so I will understand.
- Sometimes when I don't understand a word, my teacher will come up with a funny thing to help me understand it.
- She breaks words down by syllables to help me spell words easier.

Appendix A

Basic Skills Chart for Gardner's Multiple Intelligences

Intelligence	Skill with	Appreciates	Learning Productivity
Intrapersonal (self-smart)	one's own feelings, goals, anxieties planning and acting according to one's own traits	reflection meditation	journals diaries memoirs self-pacing work alone
Interpersonal (social smart)	interacting with others other people's moods, feelings, temperaments, and motivations	cooperative learning team work group work brainstorming	plays panels discussions and debates share compare interviews
Logical-Mathematical (number smart)	logical relationships relationships among actions or symbols	drills problem solving linear thinking order systematic directions mazes puzzles	count calculate demonstrate patterns experiments computer programming
Naturalist (nature smart)	important distinctions in nature	plants animals weather gardens farms natural patterns	collect classify care for/tend
Spatial-Visual (picture smart)	spatial arrays	posters videos maps charts and graphs artifacts	draw paint illustrate design photograph
Bodily-Kinesthetic (body smart)	the body as a way to solve problems or create	exercise and dance animation rhythmic movement hands-on tools	dance sports body language motor skills touch manipulatives
Linguistic (word smart)	word meanings word order sounds rhythms inflections	books stories poetry speeches author studies	write tell stories read lecture talk
Musical (music smart)	rhythm pitch meter tone melody	songs beat music videos or recordings discerning sounds	sing play an instrument perform compose music conduct music

Appendix B

Suggested Readings for Book Talk

GRADE 1

Mr. Putter and Tabby series by Cynthia Rylant—A lonely old man adopts a lonely old cat with a matching heart.

Henry and Mudge series by Cynthia Rylant—A young boy with funky parents get a huge, slobbery dog best friend.

Frog and Toad series by Arnold Lobel—Curmudgeonly Toad and Affable Frog are best buddies.

GRADE 2

The Magic Tree House series by Mary Pope Osborne—An elementary-school brother and sister have time-traveling adventures in historic settings. Read in order if possible, up through #30.

GRADE 3

Because of Winn Dixie by Kate DiCamillo—A mangy stray dog wins hearts all over town, along with the little girl who found him in the grocery store. It has wonderfully expressive "voices" and characters. After the book, there's a movie of the same title that kids can watch for a good compare/contrast conversation about which one each student prefers.

The Miraculous Journey of Edward Tulane by Kate DiCamillo—A toy rabbit has a very unusual life story that starts with him falling overboard en route to France.

The Tale of Despereaux by Kate DiCamillo—One undersized castle-dwelling mouse with one oversized brave heart and a love of music gets sent to the dungeon.

GRADES 4 AND 5

Hatchet by Gary Paulsen (Caution—preread this, as there are a few parts that might be too visual or upsetting for some students. Those sections are easily skipped.)—A twelve-year-old boy is the only survivor of a small-plane crash in the Canadian wilderness and must stay alive, hoping for rescue. This book has several sequels, but teachers should use their best judgment about using them, as each book becomes more mature. In *Hatchet*, the boy is eventually rescued before dangerous weather sets in. In the alternate-ending book, *Brian's Winter*, he has to survive a winter alone. They are both gripping adventures.

Jump Ship to Freedom by James Lincoln Collier—The Connecticut family of a free black man is wrongfully kept in bondage, and threatened with deportation to the Caribbean slave islands, until the son has a life-threatening chance to escape.

Fairytale anthologies—surprisingly appealing! Let kids choose which ones they want to hear. There are many versions of many stories. This is an easy way to read a variety of them, and to familiarize kids with American folktales compared to folktales from different countries. It helps to tell kids that most of the popular animated fairytales they may know are not always true to the original versions.

STORY BOOKS AND FICTION

Harvey Potter's Balloon Farm by Jerdine Nolan—An odd little farmer has an enticing balloon crop and a curious young neighbor.

Go, Dog. Go! By P. D. Eastman—A Seussian collection of dogs in machines that GO.

Can't You Sleep, Little Bear? by Martin Waddell and Barbara Firth—Big Bear wants to sit in his cozy cave and read his book, but Little Bear won't go to sleep.

Too Much Noise by Ann McGovern—An Eastern European folktale about a man who can't sleep in his noisy house, so seeks advice from the Holy Rabbi. Lots of fun for early grades who like to make animal noises.

The Fat Cat, A Danish Folktale by Jack Kent—A small pet cat goes on a bizarre eating rampage and grows to the size of a Macy's Thanksgiving balloon, until the local woodcutter comes along. There's a fun repetition sentence for kids.

The Relatives Came by Cynthia Rylant—A rollicking, big family reunion with lots of hugging, stories, and good food.

The Big Hungry Bear by Don and Audrey Wood—A little mouse finds a perfect strawberry just for himself until he is reminded of the big, hungry bear.

The Beast in the Bathtub by Kathleen Stevens and Ray Bowler—There's no beast under the bed or in the closet. He's in the bathtub and wants to play.

Tuesday by David Wiesner—A book without text illustrates the nighttime adventures of a frog throng flying through town on lily pads.

Mufaro's Beautiful Daughters by John Steptoe—A Cinderella story of two opposite sisters in Africa.

NONFICTION AND REALISTIC FICTION

The Bicycle Man by Allen Say—A US soldier in Japan visits an elementary school and entrances the students with his bicycle stunts.

How My Parents Learned to Eat by Ina Friedman and Allen Say—A US sailor in Japan and a local woman fall in love. They don't speak or eat the same, so they each learn the other's ways.

The Goat in the Rug by Geraldine, as told to Charles L. Blood and Martin Link—Geraldine is a very personable goat, much-loved by Glenmae, a Navajo weaver.

How Many Days to America? by Eve Bunting—A small boat of islanders escapes soldiers in their homeland, but has troubles along the way. Other soldiers finally find and help them.

New Shoes for Silvia by Johanna Hurwitz—Tia Rosita sends Silvia a pair of beautiful new red shoes, but they are too big, so Silvia has to wait wait wait to wear them.

Miss Rumphius by Barbara Cooney—A smart, spindly old lady has adventures around the world until she falls off a camel.

Sachiko Means Happiness by Sakai—A little girl helps take care of her grandmother who is fading into dementia.

Miss Maggie by Cynthia Rylant—An old woman lives alone in a decrepit shack at the edge of a farm, until a young boy befriends her.

Baseball Saved Us by Ken Mochizuki—Japanese Americans sent to an internment camp during World War II organize baseball teams and games to pass time and build a sense of community.

Hill of Fire by Thomas P. Lewis—A volcano pushes up through a Mexican farmer's cornfield.

The Other Side by Jacqueline Woodson—Clover, a young African American girl, lives next to the fence that separates the white and black sides of town. Then Annie, a visiting young white girl, sits on the fence and friendship follows.

Works by Gary Soto—Stories and books about young Hispanic kids, sports, personal journeys

Works by Laura Ingalls Wilder—Her life as a pioneer, in chapter and in picture-book formats

POETRY

Two anthologies of nonsense verse and nursery rhymes, illustrated by Wallace Tripp, full of wonderful story and discussion starters.

A Great Big Ugly Man Came Up and Tied His Horse to Me, illustrated by Wallace Tripp, and *Marguerite, Go Wash Your Feet*, illustrated by Wallace Tripp

Figure B.1. Poetry anthologies by Wallace Tripp. Created by author.

Appendix C

Project-Based Learning (PBL) Activities

Unless otherwise noted, all writing starts in the composition books.

COLLECT SOMETHING

It's good for kids not to be always on the receiving end and to know that they can contribute.

Toy drive - Students initiated a school-wide drive for Christmas presents to send to a school that was especially hard hit by recession. A large trucking company based in the state of the receiving school delivered them for free (arranged by the sending teacher with input from the receiving principal). Students wrote the blurbs for school announcements and newsletters. They sorted, boxed, and listed the donations, and wrote thank-you notes to the people/classes that helped.

Coat drive - As above, the next year, same school. The students sent all kinds of cold weather gear.

Pennies for a charity - For a local food bank

School supplies - For the school counselors in our school and other local needy buildings

Personal care items - For a staff member active in homeless causes, and a parent who worked at a veterans' hospital

Books - For a school-wide book swap

WRITE TO SOMEONE

Someone who travels - A family member took a round-trip, cross-country drive with some friends and a cat named Samson. They sent emails and pictures along the way. Students wrote captions, posted them with the pictures, and tracked both routes on a US map.

Someone far away - A school secretary's husband was the captain of a scientific ship that went from North Carolina, through the Panama Canal, along South America, to Antarctica. The class exchanged letters and pictures via email, and tracked his locations on a world map.

Museums - Almost every museum has an education specialist happy to engage with students.

An author - A group of third graders wrote to Kate DiCamillo after reading *Because of Winn-Dixie* in Book Talk. She wrote back!

Figure C.1. Maps about writing to people who travel. Created by author.

MAKE SOMETHING

Ask administration, PTA, or Student Council for funding. Items are gifts, so have boxes, wrapping paper, ribbon, bows, and gift cards. Staff folks often have extra to donate.

> *Stuffed animals* - Unstuffed shapes can be found online, so kids can choose their animals. One group invited some local firefighters to come to school and collect their stuffed animals as part of the Toys for Tots drive. Each student spoke to the firefighters. For stuffed animal patterns, visit https://www. thezoofactory.com/.

Figure C.2. Created by author.

> *Food* - (No-bake pies or cookies) *Be aware of dietary restrictions!* No-bake pumpkin pie recipes are easy to find online or in a cookbook. Substitute prepared pumpkin pie filling for canned pumpkin and spices. Pumpkin pie doesn't travel well, so it's to eat at school. One grade or class makes the pies in individual graham-cracker crusts. The pies can be refrigerated in the staff lounge or cafeteria refrigerator until it's time for students to eat them (teacher's decision). Provide plastic spoons. Kids that don't want to eat it don't have to. Extras can go to staff. The receiving groups write thank-you notes.

Figure C.3. Making pies and a class thank-you note. Created by author.

Polymer clay figures - Bears, snowmen, penguins. Use polymer clay that has to be baked. In the online example, note that the top hat is not necessary—the brim can be flattened and put on as a beret—and the scarf can be without fringe. Note, too, that black clay and red clay can stain fingers and other clay. Visit https://www.sculpey.com/create/project/sam-snowman/.

Figure C.4. Polymer clay figures and a sequential writing activity. Created by author.

Sock puppets - Inspiration is available via Sandra Boynton's YouTube video "One Shoe Blues" with B. B. King and Mom-Sock (https://www.youtube.com/watch?v=J8rLuk2PoMA). Check out the auditions for back-up socks (https://www.youtube.com/watch?v=E7TAF30Kfp0).

Materials for Mom-Sock are available at the dollar store. Scrubbies make good Mom-Sock hair. Teacher may loosely stitch or kids may use glue to assemble the puppets.

Figure C.5. Mom-Sock inspired by Sandra Boynton. Created by author.

Books and Booklets - Teacher needs a camera for illustrations in books about the community and/or the
   school. The current grade can write to incoming kids about what to expect next year or about their
   school-year favorites.

Community book:

Figure C.6. Pages from a Community booklet. Created by author.

School book:

  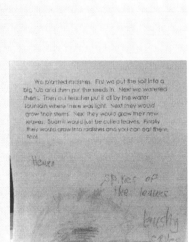

Figure C.7. Pages from School Favorites booklets. Created by author.

Houses - Make out of boxes, big or small. Kids make a list of what to make, decide who is responsible for which, then use construction paper for windows, doors, the roof, and so on.

Figure C.8. Box and construction paper houses. Created by author.

Carve a pumpkin - Kids decide and draw on the facial features and do the cleaning out. High "ew!" factor here. Teacher does all the cutting. Save the seeds to dry and have kids prepare as a snack. Teacher does the baking at home.

PLAY SOMETHING

At regular intervals or at the end of each marking period, have a "Game Day" to teach kids how to play certain board or card games. They are full of vocabulary and language for following directions, as well as taking turns and cooperative skills. As kids get proficient, or for older kids, the students can explain the game directions.

Suggested Games

Chutes and Ladders - students explain each picture they land on; cause/effect

Go Fish - using "do," "does," "have," and "has," listening and remembering

Memory/Concentration, checkers, Battleship, and (easy) Sudoku - columns, rows, left/right, up/down, prepositions of place

Trouble and Battleship - strategic thinking

Uno - strategic thinking, addition and subtraction, mental math

Jigsaw puzzles with 250 to 500 pieces - If space allows, keep one going on a back table as a quiet place or activity for kids who finish their work. Provides practice in visual tracking, fine motor, and spatial relationships.

Figure C.9. Playing games. Created by author.

Early in her career, Miss Rogers had a first-grade boy who struggled with everything. He couldn't master letter names or sounds, didn't understand basic math, and was generally losing ground. But a different kid emerged on the day the jigsaw puzzle appeared in the classroom. He could look at an incomplete puzzle, scan the pieces, and accurately find and place the right ones very quickly. It revealed a lot about how to teach him and get him to respond. He was a whiz with geo-boards, too. He was interdependent visual-spatial-tactile to the Nth degree.

Appendix D

The Great Graph

	Not very good			OK			Pretty good			Great!	
Music												
Art												
PE												
Science												
Social Studies												
Math												
Reading / Writing												

_____

_____

_____

_____

Appendix E

Comparing Proficiency Levels over Time

In Year 1, the domains are reasonably clustered at appropriate levels for an early elementary student.

In Year 2, all domains except Listening have moved up at least one level, with the typical progression of Speaking first and Writing a bit behind. This is reasonable and realistic growth, except that the gap between Listening and the other domains is widening.

In Year 3, the domains are showing steady progress with the exception of Listening. Listening is well behind the others, with the narrowest difference being over 1.5 levels. The Listening profile is far lower than it should be for a student with three years of ESOL instruction in an English-speaking school. It supports the idea that Student A has an underlying problem not related to English acquisition.

Table E.1. Year 1–Student A

	Level 1	Level 2	Level 3	Level 4	Level 5
Listening	xxxxxx	xx			
Speaking	xxxxxx	xxxxxx			
Reading	xxxxxx	xxxxxx			
Writing	xxxxxx				

Table E.2. Year 2–Student A

	Level 1	Level 2	Level 3	Level 4	Level 5
Listening	xxxxxx	xxx			
Speaking	xxxxxx	xxxxxx	xxxxxx	xx	
Reading	xxxxxx	xxxxxx	xxxxxx		
Writing	xxxxxx	xxxxxx	xx		

Table E.3. Year 3–Student A

	Level 1	Level 2	Level 3	Level 4	Level 5
Listening	xxxxxx	xxxxxx			
Speaking	xxxxxx	xxxxxx	xxxxxx	xxxxxx	xxxx
Reading	xxxxxx	xxxxxx	xxxxxx	xxxxxx	xxxx
Writing	xxxxxx	xxxxxx	xxxxxx	xxxxx	

Appendix F

Comparing Proficiency Scores within a Group

Year 1–Student B *	Level 1	Level 2	Level 3	Level 4	Level 5
Listening	xxxxx	xxxxx	xxxxx	x	
Speaking	xxxxx	xxxxx	xxxxx	xxxxx	
Reading	xxxxx	xxxx			
Writing	xxxxx				

Year 1–Student C	Level 1	Level 2	Level 3	Level 4	Level 5
Listening	xxxxx	xxxxx	xxxx		
Speaking	xxxxx	xxxxx	xxxxx		
Reading	xxxxx	xxxxx			
Writing	xxxxx	xxx			

Year 1–Student D	Level 1	Level 2	Level 3	Level 4	Level 5
Listening	xxxxx	xxxxx			
Speaking	xxxxx	xxxxx			
Reading	xxxxx	xxxx			
Writing	xxxxx	xxxxx			

Year 3–Student B *	Level 1	Level 2	Level 3	Level 4	Level 5
Listening	xxxxx	xxxxx	xxxxx	xxxxx	xxxxx
Speaking	xxxxx	xxxxx	xxxxx	xxxxx	xxxxx
Reading	xxxxx	xxxxx	xx		
Writing	xxxxx	xxx			

Year 3–Student C	Level 1	Level 2	Level 3	Level 4	Level 5
Listening	xxxxx	xxxxx	xxxxx	xxxxx	xxxxx
Speaking	xxxxx	xxxxx	xxxxx	xxxxx	xxxxx
Reading	xxxxx	xxxxx	xxxxx	xxxxx	xxxx
Writing	xxxxx	xxxxx	xxxxx	xxxxx	xxx

Year 3–Student D	Level 1	Level 2	Level 3	Level 4	Level 5
Listening	xxxxx	xxxxx	xxxxx	xxxxx	xxxxx
Speaking	xxxxx	xxxxx	xxxxx	xxxxx	xxxxx
Reading	xxxxx	xxxxx	xxxxx	xxxxx	xxxxx
Writing	xxxxx	xxxxx	xxxxx	xxxxx	xxxxx

The students start at appropriate levels, with reasonable spread among the domains. Student B's domains become widely discrepant while the other two students make regular growth across the board. Student B's Reading and Writing are significantly behind Student B's Speaking and Listening, and way behind the peers' scores. Intra- and inter-student discrepancies strongly suggest a non-ESOL learning problem.

Index

technology for the unemployed, 42–43
TESOL. *See* teachers of English for speakers of other languages
testing English proficiency, 17, 26, 73
text size, 28
time in country, 70–71
total physical response (TPR), xiv, 77
Tripp, Wallace, 87

undocumented people, 3
United States (U.S.): corporate punishment in, 11; emigres to, 2; first generation students in, 9; immigrants jobs in, 7; level 1–2 beginner and, 18; non-English speakers in, 1

Valenstein, Erica, 79
Vietnam, xv, 18, 70–71
Vincent (student), 74
visual aids, 31

Wagstaff, Janiel M., 42
Wainwright, Robb, 78–79
websites: for American hand gestures, 11; for cultural differences, 9; of Department of Education, 2, 17; for English for speakers of other languages, 42–43; for Maryland public television graphic organizers, 65–66; for nonfiction summaries templates, 60; Omniglot, 16; for Purdue online writing lab, 65
work samples, 73–74
World English, xiv, 1, 8
writing, 16, 49–50, 89, 91; as domains, xiii, 15; Dots Write for, 61, 62–63; general organization of, 62–63; kids piece of, 65–66; level 1–2 beginners and, 19; level 3–4 intermediates and, 22–23; level 5–6 advanced and, 23–24; point of view for, 64; summaries for, 59–62

Yogi (student), xvi

Zammillo, Amanda, 78

About the Author

Ann Morgan is a long-time elementary and ESOL teacher, teacher trainer, and writer with experience at all levels of English language acquisition in K–8 and college. She holds multiple master's degrees and has worked as a writer, editor, and/or consultant for the state of Maryland, Oxford University Press, the Library of Congress, Discovery Education, and the National Institutes of Health.

24536556R00071

Made in the USA
San Bernardino, CA
06 February 2019